M000238608

STEPS

GOSPEL-CENTERED RECOVERY

Leader Guide

MATT CHANDLER
MICHAEL SNETZER

LifeWay Press®
Nashville, Tennessee

Published by LifeWay Press® • © 2015 The Village Church • Reprinted 2019

No part of this book may be reproduced or transmitted in any form or by any means, electronic or mechanical, including photocopying and recording, or by any information storage or retrieval system, except as may be expressly permitted in writing by the publisher. Requests for permission should be addressed in writing to LifeWay Press®; One LifeWay Plaza; Nashville, TN 37234.

ISBN 978-1-4300-3215-1 • Item 005644098
Dewey decimal classification: 248.84 • Subject headings: DISCIPLESHIP / CHRISTIAN LIFE / SIN

Unless indicated otherwise, Scripture quotations are taken from The Holy Bible, English Standard Version® (ESV®), copyright © 2001 by Crossway, a publishing ministry of Good News Publishers. Used by permission. All rights reserved. Scripture quotations marked NIV are taken from the Holy Bible, NEW INTERNATIONAL VERSION®. Copyright © 1973, 1978, 1984 by Biblica Inc. All rights reserved worldwide. Used by permission.

To order additional copies of this resource, write to LifeWay Resources Customer Service; One LifeWay Plaza; Nashville, TN 37234; fax 615-251-5933; order online at LifeWay.com; phone toll free 800-458-2772; or email orderentry@lifeway.com.

Printed in the United States of America

Groups Ministry Publishing • LifeWay Resources • One LifeWay Plaza • Nashville, TN 37234

Contents

Introduction to *Steps* Discipleship

> Jesus came and said to them, "All authority in heaven and on earth
> has been given to me. Go therefore and make disciples of all nations,
> baptizing them in the name of the Father and of the Son and of the
> Holy Spirit, teaching them to observe all that I have commanded you.
> And behold, I am with you always, to the end of the age."
>
> **MATTHEW 28:18-20**

The mission of *Steps* fits into the church's greater mission of bringing glory to God by making disciples through gospel-centered worship, gospel-centered community, gospel-centered service, and gospel-centered multiplication. *Steps* is an intensive discipleship program that consists of daily Bible study and reflection, one-on-one mentoring, sharing in small groups, and a large-group teaching time.

We should not view *Steps* as an attempt to climb a staircase to God through a religious system but rather as steps of obedience in faithful response to what God has already accomplished and promised through the gospel of Jesus Christ.

> No one can lay a foundation other than that which is laid, which is
> Jesus Christ. Now if anyone builds on the foundation with gold, silver,
> precious stones, wood, hay, straw—each one's work will become
> manifest, for the Day will disclose it, because it will be revealed by
> fire, and the fire will test what sort of work each one has done.
>
> **1 CORINTHIANS 3:11-13**

Many people in our culture claim to be Christians but have never heard a comprehensive gospel message. *Steps* begins by laying the foundation of what Jesus has accomplished on the cross for those who believe (gospel truths) and then bids people to live out the call to follow Christ (gospel pursuits).

Part of the sanctification process is examining our hearts before the Lord. In *Steps* we refer to this as assessment. Assessment involves confession and prayer about the fruit of our lives and its roots. We bring all this before the Lord so that He can uproot our sinful patterns and heal our hearts, freeing us to act faithfully for His kingdom.

On the missional front we first engage with the traditional 12 Steps. But to clarify, we are not trying to legitimize the traditional 12 Steps. Instead, we will examine and deconstruct each step, claim whatever truth it may hold, reconstruct the step within a biblical framework, and apply it within a gospel context.

For freedom Christ has set us free; stand firm therefore,
and do not submit again to a yoke of slavery.
GALATIANS 5:1

KNOW THE WORD, DO THE WORD

The message of the gospel is both comfort and call. It presents the comforting truth that in Christ we have been forgiven and made righteous. We are now sons and daughters of God and accepted into His kingdom for eternity, not because of any worth or work of our own but because of the loving choice of the Father and the sacrifice of the Son.

The gospel also offers us, as citizens of the kingdom, a call—a call to come and die, to forsake everything for the expansion of the kingdom of God, and to push back what is dark in the world. This call bids us to throw off the old self and clothe ourselves with the new self.

The structure of *Steps* addresses both the comfort and the call of the gospel message. Weeks 1–4 proclaim gospel truths (comfort), while weeks 5–12 begin to incorporate the importance of gospel pursuits (call).

WEEKS 1–4

- The nature and character of God
- The fall
- Redemption
- Grace
- Faith and justification
- Adoption
- Sanctification
- Future glory

WEEKS 5–12

- Holiness
- Reconciliation
- Spiritual disciplines
- Making disciples
- Gospel-centered worship
- Gospel-centered community
- Gospel-centered service
- Gospel-centered multiplication

FIVE PARTS OF STEPS

1. SMALL GROUPS

Relationships are necessary components to our spiritual growth. We strongly recommend that each person entering *Steps* be in biblical community. During the first hour of each week's group session, participants are divided into small groups by gender. These small groups range in size but ideally have no more than 12 participants. These groups begin with prayer, after which the group leader guides discussion. We encourage relationships begun in the groups to grow outside the groups. This happens when participants get together outside their small groups to encourage one another and to grow into deeper relationships.

2. TEACHING

The final hour is spent in the large group viewing a related video teaching for the week's study.

3. MENTORS

Mentors are believers who have faithfully completed the *Steps* program and the necessary training and have developed sufficient spiritual maturity to disciple someone else. Participants and mentors are responsible to meet together weekly. It is one thing to guide someone through a program; it is a much different thing to encourage others in their relationship with Christ and to teach all He has commanded His followers. It is important for a mentor to be able to do both.

4. DAILY STUDY

Daily homework—a combination of Bible study, reflection, and prayer—is required throughout the *Steps* program. In addition, "Going Deeper" questions are designed to challenge participants to honestly and prayerfully examine their lives in light of the Scriptures they are studying. Participants then bring these reflections to their leader and share what the Lord has revealed. This process will obviously be uncomfortable for some participants, but over time it will build intimacy within a safe environment.

5. ASSESSMENT

In the middle of the program (weeks 5–7), we will transition from homework to assessment work. This is a time of reflecting on and writing about specific sins, situations, and relationships that may be robbing us of the freedom we have in Christ. At the end of this period, the study returns to the devotional-style homework.

Leader Role, Expectations, and Accountability

BEING A SHEPHERD LEADER

Anyone even vaguely familiar with the biblical narrative will recognize the rather dominant theme of shepherding. Exodus 3:1 states that Moses "was keeping the flock of his father-in-law." Moses was a shepherd.

Scripture includes a number of references to shepherding and men of faith who are described this way. Abel was a shepherd, as were Abraham, Jacob, and David, just to name a few of the Old Testament figures with that responsibility. God Himself is called a Shepherd in a number of significant passages, which consequently refer to His people as sheep: Psalm 23; 78:52; Isaiah 40:11; Ezekiel 34:11-13; John 10:11; 1 Peter 2:25.

Within the pages of the New Testament, the picture continues as Jesus called His apostles to be shepherds of the church. See particularly Jesus' charge to Peter in John 21. The apostles then gave this charge to the elders of local churches, who apparently appointed various shepherds within the congregation (see Eph. 4:11). While certain positions (pastors, group leaders, etc.) carry an inherent responsibility to guard the flock, every believer in some sense functions as a shepherd. We are all called to watch over our families, our own lives, our friends, etc.

Not many of us are consumed with thoughts of sheep unless possibly we are trying to sleep. It will be helpful, then, to provide a brief overview of the responsibilities that come with this calling. Shepherds are called to feed, protect, lead, and discipline the flock with which they have been entrusted.

RESPONSIBILITIES OF A SHEPHERD LEADER

- Feed God's sheep (see John 21:15-17; 1 Cor. 3:2).
- Protect from predators and lies (see Matt. 7:15; Heb. 5:14).
- Lead by example (see 1 Cor. 11:1).
- Discipline in order to bring sheep back into the flock (see Luke 15:3-7; Jas. 5:19-20).

THE CHARACTER OF A SHEPHERD LEADER

- Use the Scriptures (see Ps. 119:115; 2 Tim. 3:16).
- Point to and love Jesus as the Good Shepherd (see John 10:1-8, 1 Pet. 2:25).

- Love people with compassion and challenge (see Luke 10:25-37; 1 Thess. 5:14; 1 John 4:19).
- Willingness to enter into difficult circumstances (see 1 Sam. 17:31-37; Luke 15:1-7).

THE WORK OF A SHEPHERD LEADER

Each week, after you have met with those who have been entrusted to your care, you will be asked to assess your leadership and how you sought to foster biblical community. Each week you will be asked to revisit these two tethers, specifically applying these foundational attributes of the work.

BEING A SHEPHERD LEADER

- Care (genuine, authentic, safe, intentional)
- Encourage (to maturity, in understanding and applying the gospel)
- Model (Christ, joy in Christ)
- Mobilize (to be a part of biblical community, to fulfill their role in serving in the body of Christ)

FOSTERING BIBLICAL COMMUNITY

- Grace
- Generosity
- Diversity
- Care
- Humility
- Unity

An Overview of Biblical Counseling

The following overview seeks to differentiate biblical counseling from other forms of counsel that the world offers. Because we bear an influence on the lives that God has entrusted to us as shepherds, we must ensure that our counsel is biblical. Biblical counseling is distinct because it is rooted in the Scriptures, is aimed at the heart with the gospel of Jesus Christ, and exhorts Christ followers with the greatest command.

ROOTED IN THE SCRIPTURES

> Where is the one who is wise? Where is the scribe? Where is the debater of this age? Has not God made foolish the wisdom of the world?
> **1 CORINTHIANS 1:20**

> The words of the wise are like goads, and like nails firmly fixed are the collected sayings; they are given by one Shepherd. My son, beware of anything beyond these.
> **ECCLESIASTES 12:11-12**

THE WISDOM OF GOD VERSUS THE WISDOM OF THE WORLD

Rightly understood, all wisdom can be categorized in one of two ways. The Bible defines these sources of wisdom as the wisdom of God and the wisdom of the world (see 1 Cor 1:20-21). These two sources of wisdom are actually two different worldviews. One worldview exalts God and His glory as utmost; the other elevates man and his concerns. These two viewpoints regard the other as foolish and stand in opposition to each other. Even some Christians have tried to find a middle ground between these two worldviews. Biblical counseling begins from a perspective rooted in the wisdom of God and is oriented around His glory.

The wisdom of God is displayed most clearly in Jesus Christ. All creation exists to bring Him glory. The wisdom of the world reinterprets our experiences and desires in a way that leads us away from God as we orient our lives primarily around ourselves. The wisdom of the world is limited because it is based in speculation. The wisdom of God is based in revelation. As such, all counsel that group leaders provide should be rooted in the wisdom God has revealed in His Word.

THE RELATIONSHIP BETWEEN ROOT AND FRUIT

Thus says the LORD:
"Cursed is the man who trusts in man
and makes flesh his strength,
whose heart turns away from the LORD.
He is like a shrub in the desert,
and shall not see any good come.
He shall dwell in the parched places of the wilderness,
in an uninhabited salt land.
Blessed is the man who trusts in the LORD,
whose trust is the LORD.
He is like a tree planted by water,
that sends out its roots by the stream,
and does not fear when heat comes,
for its leaves remain green,
and is not anxious in the year of drought,
for it does not cease to bear fruit."

JEREMIAH 17:5-8

As can be seen in the previous passage, the two responses Jeremiah described lead to radically different lives. One is fruitful, and the other is fruitless. The fruit of a person's life will reveal their foundation. Those who put their trust in God and His Word are nourished by the living waters of Jesus Christ. Their lives will be characterized by peace and good fruit amid difficult circumstances. Those who trust in man and the world will experience chaos and desolation. Those who seek to counsel biblically will encourage trust and faith in God with the understanding that faithful obedience to the Lord flows from a heart reconciled to Him by faith in Jesus.

AIMED AT THE HEART

The heart is deceitful above all things
and desperately sick;
who can understand it?

JEREMIAH 17:9

TARGETING SYMPTOMS OR ROOT CAUSES

The Bible describes the heart as the seat of a person, from which our emotions, thoughts, and behaviors originate (see Mark 7:21-22). The heart is the wellspring of our lives that drives our motivations and desires. Because of sin our hearts are corrupt. Outside the gospel we live with an incurable spiritual heart disease. By God's grace, faith in Jesus brings a new heart with new desires. However, sin and its effects remain, hindering our ability to see God, ourselves, and our lives rightly. Therefore, we need counsel that addresses the fundamental commitments in our lives with the hope of the gospel.

Secular approaches to counseling often treat only symptoms, focusing on behavior, thoughts, and emotions while failing to address the deeper issues of the heart. Treating symptoms has been described as giving aspirin to someon for a headache caused by a brain tumor. It may relieve the headache for a time, but it does nothing to fix the brain tumor.

Thankfully, we are not left without hope. God understands our hearts and has given us insights in His Word to explain the inner workings of man. God pursues the hearts of His people and will not rest until He wins them entirely. The biblical counsel that group leaders provide should address the root causes of our problems, not our symptoms alone.

THE GOSPEL OF JESUS CHRIST

To those who are called, both Jews and Greeks,
Christ [is] the power of God and the wisdom of God.
1 CORINTHIANS 1:24

The gospel of Jesus Christ is the unfolding plan of God to redeem a people for His glory. God's Word reveals that the cause of all human suffering is sin. Therefore, the counsel that group leaders provide exalts the supremacy of the gospel of Jesus Christ as our ultimate hope amid our sin and suffering. To that end we seek to connect the truths of the gospel to our everyday struggles so that we can rejoice in the transformative grace of Jesus.

EXHORTING WITH THE GREATEST COMMAND

"Hear, O Israel: The Lord our God, the Lord is one. And you shall love the Lord your God with all your heart and with all your soul and with all your mind and with all your strength." The second is this: "You shall love your neighbor as yourself." There is no commandment greater than these.
MARK 12:29-31

God has hardwired us for worship. It is an expression of our humanness. We worship what is uppermost in our affections. The question is not whether we worship but what we worship.

All sin stems from disordered desires. These desires lead to idolatry—the worship of anything other than God. When we sin, we declare that in that moment we love something more than we love God. We give worship that is rightly due Him to another.

Through the gospel we are given new hearts with the reordering of His creative design and the reorientation of our hearts in worship to Him. Gospel-centered worship is a response to the reality that in Christ we have been given all things—the greatest of these being God Himself. Biblical counsel exhorts Christians to pursue rightly ordered worship that spills over into faithful action. We are to be "doers of the word, and not hearers only" (Jas. 1:22).

BIBLICAL COUNSELING EXAMPLE: DEPRESSION

How can these elements of biblical counseling be applied to serious problems like depression? To think biblically about depression, we must first begin by developing a biblical anthropology, or a scriptural understanding of people and what influences them. From this we will see that while it is possible to be spiritually oppressed, physically defective, and pressed by the circumstances around us, we can respond by the Holy Spirit with trust and faith in Christ under God's sovereign rule.

A Biblical Anthropology of the Active and the Passive Heart

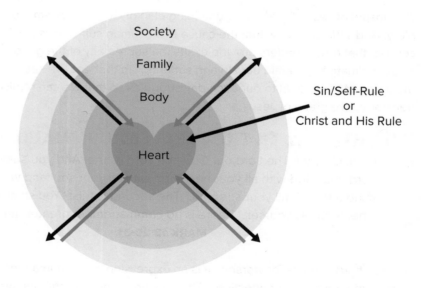

Society

Family

Body

Heart

Sin/Self-Rule
or
Christ and His Rule

John Henderson, *Equipped to Counsel* (Bedford, TX: Association of Biblical Counselors, 2008).

From the diagram we see that there are physiological, social, and spiritual realities that can influence a person. Our physical bodies, the societies and cultures in which we live, and the unseen spiritual realm all influence our lives. Yet above it all God sits sovereignly enthroned, fully in control. He is sovereign over all things. Therefore, if we trust God in the midst of a chaotic situation, we will bear good fruit regardless of the source of the difficulty (see Jer. 17:7-8). If we place our trust elsewhere, we will be:

> like a shrub in the desert
> and shall not see any good come.
> **JEREMIAH 17:6**

This truth hints at the greater reality present as we counsel those who are struggling with depression. Despite the influences that surround us, the Bible focuses on the heart as the center of emotion, intellect, will, and desire. It is at the heart level that God ministers His grace to sufferers of depression.

One of the common features of depression is hopelessness. As you listen to others' stories of depression, you often hear evidence of misplaced hope. Many who struggle with depression say they have nothing left to live for. Their desires and dreams have gone unsatisfied. They feel lifeless, plunged into darkness. They have lost hope, motivation, and purpose. What a place for the gospel to enter!

In the greatest commandment Jesus exhorts us not to place our hope in lesser loves (see Mark 12:30). This is both for His glory and our good. In contrast to Jesus' words, depression often results from putting our hope in something other than God and His promise of redemption through the gospel of Jesus Christ. Because the world as we know it is passing away, finding our meaning in this world and the people of this world will leave us like Solomon, who, having it all, exclaimed, "Meaningless! Meaningless! ... Everything is meaningless! ... a chasing after the wind" (Eccl. 1:1-14, NIV).

We are told in Matthew 6:33:

> Seek first the kingdom of God and His righteousness,
> and all these things will be added to you.
> **MATTHEW 6:33**

In our natural, sinful state we seek the things we love—what we treasure. Jesus warns us that to treasure the things of the earth is to grasp for temporary, fleeting things that can never deliver on the security they promise. Instead, we are called to treasure and seek the eternal things of the kingdom of heaven.

We seek with our eyes, so if our eye is bad (when we seek temporary hopes and treasures), our whole body will be full of darkness. How great is that darkness outside the hope of the gospel! But if our eye is full of light, it brings light to the whole body. Through the gospel we have been given the eternal riches of the Kingdom. If someone is depressed, we want to invite that person to know the only One who brings light to the darkness, life from the dead, and order from chaos.

Even if there is a true chemical imbalance caused by a physical problem in our bodies or if there is spiritual oppression or social anxiety, our ministry to depressed people remains the same. We compassionately minister to the heart with the hope of the gospel of Jesus Christ amid all circumstances. There has never been a case of chemical imbalance (other than Jesus sweating blood in the garden of Gethsemane) that did not also expose heart issues that needed to be addressed.

This does not mean we discourage helpful symptomatic relief through medication or other means. It means we never want to lose sight that our real hope is not a chemical or a feeling. As Paul Tripp has said, "Hope is a person, and his name is Jesus Christ."[1] No matter how terrible a person feels, it is possible to look on our lives and situation with hope because of the light of the gospel of Jesus Christ.

These truths do not minimize or discount the very real and deep darkness of depression. God sees, and He cares. Because God is sovereign, He takes us into difficult seasons and uses them for good. There is a purpose for our suffering. Often the heart is exposed in seemingly never-ending forms of pride and idolatry, but through the gospel there is unending grace as God rescues us from the bondage of lesser hopes.

PLEASE NOTE: Additional Assessment Training can be downloaded from disc 1 of *Steps Bible Study Kit* or at *lifeway.com/steps*.

The Assessment Process

LEADING YOUR GROUP THROUGH THE ASSESSMENT

The assessment process includes both the rooting out of sin and the replanting of truth.

The goal in assessment is not for participants to identify every sin they have ever committed but to illuminate dysfunctional (sinful) patterns of relating to God and others. We want to be free of the things that rob our affections for Christ and hinder our ability to live for His kingdom purposes. Through this process we want to teach participants how to examine their hearts.

It is important to root ourselves in the gospel as we examine the darkness of our hearts. We begin by standing in the truths of the gospel—what Christ accomplished, what He is accomplishing, and what He promises to accomplish. We ask the Holy Spirit to reveal areas that hinder us from properly relating to God and others as ambassadors to a lost and dying world. We spend time writing what He reveals in our assessment. We must continually remember the gospel, believe the gospel, and stand in the gospel so that the Enemy does not cause us to stumble.

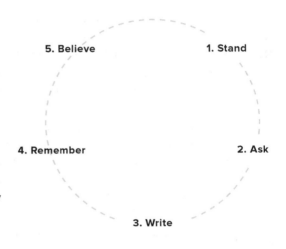

5. Believe

1. Stand

4. Remember

2. Ask

3. Write

ASSESSMENT IS:
- Examining our hearts, guided by the Holy Spirit
- Being able to identify our sins and the sinful patterns behind them

ASSESSMENT IS NOT:
- An attempt to document every sin
- A one-time event

ASSESSMENT FORMS

The assessment forms are modified and expanded from forms in *Joe and Charlie Big Book Study,* then viewed through a redemptive lens.

THE PROCESS OF ASSESSMENT

PHASE 1: *Examine Fruit*

In phase 1 participants should fill out the assessment forms. The forms illuminate the fruit of a person's thoughts, actions, and beliefs. There are six forms: Abuse, Resentment, Guilt & Shame, Sexual Immorality, Fear, and Grief.

> When you were slaves of sin, you were free in regard to righteousness.
> But what fruit were you getting at that time from the things of which you
> are now ashamed? For the end of those things is death. But now that you
> have been set free from sin and have become slaves of God, the fruit you
> get leads to sanctification and its end, eternal life. For the wages of sin
> is death, but the free gift of God is eternal life in Christ Jesus our Lord.
> **ROMANS 6:20-23**

Traditional step 4: We made a searching and fearless moral assessment of ourselves.

Redeemed truth from step 4: As children of God armed with the Holy Spirit and standing firm in the gospel, we engage in the spiritual battle over the reign and rule of our hearts. God set us apart for holiness, and we look to put to death the areas of our lives that keep us from reflecting Jesus Christ to a dark and dying world. We first examine the fruit in our lives (or moral symptoms). As we move through the assessment process, we will uncover the roots of any ungodly fruit (pride and idolatry) that drive our ungodly thoughts, actions, and emotions.

PHASE 2: *Confess and Pray*

> If we say we have fellowship with him while we walk in darkness,
> we lie and do not practice the truth. But if we walk in the light,
> as he is in the light, we have fellowship with one another,
> and the blood of Jesus his Son cleanses us from all sin.
> **1 JOHN 1:6-7**

Traditional step 5: We admitted before God, ourselves, and another human being the exact nature of our wrongs.

Redeemed truth from step 5: Under the covering of God's grace, we step out in faith, leaving behind our old, self-protective ways of covering sin and hiding from God. We prayerfully come into the light, confessing our sins before God and to one another so that we may be healed.

As participants confess each item on the assessment, mentors should use the prayer prompts to help them pray about each issue or person. We have also provided two pages for taking notes. We recommend that mentors take notes while reviewing each section of the assessment.

PHASE 3: *Expose Roots*

> If the root is holy, so are the branches.
> **ROMANS 11:16**

By examining the various columns on each assessment form, mentors will help participants uncover roots of pride, idolatry, and spiritual adultery that are causing the sinful fruit of their lives.

PHASE 4: *Replanting Truth and Renouncing Lies*
This phase of assessment deals with the spiritual dynamics behind the character defects, lies, and vows we consciously or unconsciously believed, pronounced, or entered.

> ... assuming that you have heard about him and were taught in him,
> as the truth is in Jesus, to put off your old self, which belongs to
> your former manner of life and is corrupt through deceitful desires.
> **EPHESIANS 4:21-22**

Traditional step 6: We are entirely ready to have God remove all these defects of character.

Traditional step 7: We humbly asked Him to remove our shortcomings.

Redeemed truth from steps 6 & 7: In attempting to live independent of God, we have developed dysfunctional (sinful) patterns of coping. After careful examination we have begun to see the demonic roots of our slavery to these sinful patterns. We desire freedom. We renounce our former ways; offer ourselves to God; and, under the waterfall of His grace, ask Him to deliver and heal us by the authority of Christ and the power of the Holy Spirit. We also pray for blessing and the empowerment of the Holy Spirit to live life according to His kingdom purposes.

Using the sample guide provided, mentors will help participants identify these lies, vows, and sinful patterns and then pray with them.

PHASE 5: *Encourage to Faithful Action*

Through confession, prayer, counsel, and deliverance, participants have worked to expel the sins, wounds, and oppressive powers that hinder their ability to "walk in a manner worthy of the Lord." Mentors will encourage participants toward reconciliation, community, and obedience.

> Walk in a manner worthy of the Lord, fully pleasing to him, bearing
> fruit in every good work and increasing in the knowledge of God.
> **COLOSSIANS 1:10**

Traditional step 8: We made a list of all persons we had harmed and became willing to make amends to them all.

Traditional step 9: We made direct amends to such people whenever possible, except when to do so would injure them or others.

Redeemed truth from steps 8 & 9: Relationships break down because of sin. If there were no sin in the world, relationships would work harmoniously, evidenced by love and unity. Division among God's people provides opportunities to identify sin and purify the body. The gospel of Jesus Christ brings about justice in a way that the law cannot by inwardly reconciling the very heart of injustice to God. As those forgiven by God, we can humbly approach those affected by our sin and make amends. This change of heart brings glory to God by demonstrating the power of the gospel and reflecting His heart in bringing justice through His reconciled people.

Traditional step 10: We continued to take personal inventory and, when we were wrong, promptly admitted it.

Traditional step 11: We sought through prayer and meditation to improve our conscious contact with God, praying only for the knowledge of His will and the power to carry that out.

Redeemed truth from steps 10 & 11: We continue in the fear of the Lord, putting to death those things that rob our affections for Christ while persevering in our loving and joyful obedience to Him. We return to the Lord quickly with an attitude of repentance, when out of step with the Spirit, as we're trained in godliness and grow spiritually. Since He is our ultimate treasure, we seek to know Him and fill ourselves with those things that stir our affections for Him. We practice spiritual disciplines so that our hearts, so prone to wander, might stay in rhythm with His.

Traditional step 12: Having had a spiritual experience as the result of these steps, we try to carry this message to others and to practice these principles in all our affairs.

Redeemed truth from step 12: Before the foundations of the earth, God chose us, the church, to live as messengers of reconciliation to a lost and dying world, bearing witness to His wisdom and power through the gospel of Jesus Christ. It is our joy-filled worship to make much of His name, empowered by the Holy Spirit in bringing a comprehensive gospel demonstrated by our deeds and proclaimed by our words, with the goal of making disciples for Jesus Christ. In this same way, we incarnate Christ, being His hands and feet on the earth.

SEEKING RECONCILIATION AND AMENDS

The work of amends displays God as a just God who cares about His children and is intent on bringing justice to the oppressed. We arrive at this justice through the reconciliation of our hearts to His through the gospel of grace, which cures what the law cannot. The gospel alone transforms the heart of injustice.

The light of Christ shines into our hearts. It exposes darkness while providing the hope of restoration through the reconciling work of Jesus Christ. He Himself demonstrates the power and possibility of overcoming sin, suffering, and death. For those of us who are forgiven by God and are now living as His ambassadors, this process allows us to bring light and hope to a dark world. We are to use all of our energy and resources to glorify His name. Confessing our wrongs with a sincere desire to make things right is an opportunity to testify to the character of God as both just and merciful. Restitution is often a forgotten component of repentance; however, a repentant heart, in response to God's grace, is willing to forsake any worldly costs because of the promise of Christ for all eternity.

WILLINGNESS VERSUS WISDOM

With respect to making amends, step 8 speaks to willingness, and step 9 speaks to wisdom. We must be willing to make amends but use wisdom in making them. For example, it might not be wise to make direct amends in dangerous situations. It might not be wise to look up every person you have ever had a sexual experience with and invite them to coffee. It might not be wise to meet with a married person of the opposite sex without his or her spouse. You should use wisdom and sensitivity in the words you choose and consider your audience in acknowledging your wrongs. It might not be wise to confess sinful thoughts or attitudes to someone who is unaware that you thought of them that way. It might not be wise to force an amends before a person is willing to receive it. Remember, the Holy Spirit leads. He will impress on you whom to approach, direct you when to approach, and may even bring some unexpected opportunities to make peace.

The exception—"except when to do so would injure them or others"—is often used as a cover-up for unwillingness. For example, we should not use this exception as an excuse not to confess adultery, claiming it would hurt the other person too much. Confession allows true healing to occur rather than covering up the sin that disrupts fellowship. As long as secrets remain, we cannot have true fellowship. If we do not confess adultery, a marriage is based on deceit. In confessing situations that include sexual sin, consider sparing the other person specific details that may make healing unnecessarily difficult.

A TEMPLATE FOR MAKING AMENDS

Peacemaker Ministries suggests the seven A's of confession, which we adapted for *Steps:*
1. Address those affected.
2. Avoid excusing your wrongs or being overly dramatic in an attempt to evoke pity.
3. Admit specific attitudes and actions.
4. Acknowledge the hurt and express regret for harm caused.
5. Accept the consequences and be willing to make restitution.
6. Accompany confession with altered attitudes and actions.
7. Ask for forgiveness.[2]

Example: "I am grateful that God has granted me this opportunity to speak with you today. The gospel of Jesus Christ has had a profound effect on my life. He has both provided me hope and exposed the depths of my sin. In light of His work in my life, I deeply regret how my sinful attitudes and actions have affected you. I am here to ask for your forgiveness. [Explain how you wronged this person.] I regret the harm I have caused you. I know I cannot heal the wounds I have caused, but I serve a God who can. Will you forgive me? What can I do to make this situation right?"

Often we already know what we need to do to make things right. If we owe someone money, we may be prepared to pay them with interest. Sometimes we are not in a position to make full restitution at that point, but we can give something and make arrangements for future payments.

For those of us who have misused religion, the Bible, or God to justify a sinful attitude or behavior, it is wise to acknowledge ways we have been wrong.

EXAMPLES OF RESTITUTION

Relational: In rebellion against God's created order, we have lived for ourselves and have used people for our selfish desires. Now that we are reconciled to God, we desire to make amends for harm done through our selfish ambitions.

Legal: At times our self-seeking behavior has led us not only to rebel against God but also to break laws intended to uphold and safeguard society. Setting things right may mean making amends and possibly restitution for harm done.

Professional: We may not have been faithful to the responsibilities entrusted to us professionally.

Financial: Monetary compensation may be required to make things right.

Religious/spiritual: We may need to confess and ask for forgiveness for misleading someone spiritually.

Living: A person may not be willing to hear from us, in which case we must demonstrate the transformative effects of the gospel in our lives by living faithfully and responsibly.

PURSUING JOY IN CHRIST

> Behold, a lawyer stood up to put him to the test, saying, "Teacher, what shall I do to inherit eternal life?" He said to him, "What is written in the Law? How do you read it?" And he answered, "You shall love the Lord your God with all your heart and with all your soul and with all your strength and with all your mind, and your neighbor as yourself."
> **LUKE 10:25-27**

There is no template or to-do list that will lead to fullness of life other than obedience to the incarnate Word of God, as directed by the Holy Spirit, rooted in love for the person and work of Jesus Christ. Scripture tells us:

> In Christ Jesus neither circumcision nor uncircumcision counts for anything, but only faith working through love.
> **GALATIANS 5:6**

For each person, faith must express itself in action done from a regenerate heart of love for Jesus. These are not works to become righteous but rather are expressions of the new heart and righteousness given to us in Christ.

LOVING GOD (VERTICAL)

- Meeting with God through the spiritual disciplines so that we can know Him and the power of His resurrection
- Expressions of gratitude—enjoying His gifts, joining His ministry, and serving in His church
- Stoking the flames of gospel-motivated worship—expressions of the heart, both individually and corporately
- Obedience to His statutes—learning, doing, and sharing with others
- Continued mortification of sin

LOVING OTHERS AND SELF (HORIZONTAL)

- Making disciples for Christ
- Reflecting the heart of God and the mind of Christ
- Gospel-centered service
- Gospel-empowered ministry and mission
- Gospel-saturated community
- Seeking reconciliation for sins committed
- Taking care of your body, the temple of God
- Asking your Father in heaven for what you need

Mentors and participants should agree on a plan of action for seeking reconciliation and amends. This includes making a list of people whom participants owe amends or forgiveness.

Some other ideas for pursuing joy in Christ:

- Key Scriptures to combat lies, unbelief, and fears; an ongoing study and meditation plan
- Instruction in prayer and the pursuit of biblical community
- Helping participants consider, plan, and ask the Lord how He can utilize them in making disciples

Format Options

There are two options for the format of your weekly gathering during the *Steps* discipleship process. This book provides viewer guides for taking notes on the video teaching at the beginning of each week. Most groups will choose to show the videos first (the first option below), but either format can be effective.

I. VIDEO TEACHING IS SHOWN BEFORE GROUP MEMBERS COMPLETE THE RELATED HOMEWORK

VIDEO, PERSONAL DAYS 1–6 + GOING DEEPER, GROUP DISCUSSION

In this format personal study or assessments completed during the week will be based on truths introduced in the video teaching shown in the previous group session.

Mentors will meet with individuals during the week to discuss the Going Deeper questions and/or assessments. Ideally, individuals and mentors will meet weekly throughout *Steps,* but it is vital that these one-on-one meetings occur at least during the assessment process.

Each small-group session will then begin with prayer and discussion to review the personal study completed during the week. Then the group will watch the next video, which will introduce a new topic to be studied during the following week and discussed at the beginning of the next group session.

NOTE: Video teaching may be shown in small groups, or if multiple groups are meeting at the same time and location, everyone may meet together to watch the video and have a time of worship. If the videos are shown in small groups, you may choose to have brief discussion following the teaching to highlight key points and gather initial reactions from group members.

2. VIDEO TEACHING IS SHOWN AFTER GROUP MEMBERS COMPLETE THE RELATED HOMEWORK

PERSONAL DAYS 1–6 + GOING DEEPER, GROUP DISCUSSION, VIDEO

In this format personal study or assessments completed during the week will explore truths in preparation for the video teaching shown in the upcoming group session.

Mentors will meet with individuals during the week to discuss the Going Deeper questions and/or assessments. Ideally, individuals and mentors will meet weekly throughout *Steps,* but it is vital that these one-on-one meetings occur at least during the assessment process.

Each group session will begin with prayer and discussion to review the personal study completed during the week. Then the group will watch the related video to conclude the topic studied and discussed.

NOTE: Video teaching may be shown in small groups, or if multiple groups are meeting at the same time and location, everyone may meet together to watch the video and have a time of worship. If the videos are shown in small groups, you may choose to have brief discussion following the teaching to highlight key points and gather initial reactions from group members.

Over time your church may choose to do live teaching instead of using the videos, in which case you will not use the viewer guides provided.

Leader and Mentor Training

Each time your church offers *Steps,* plan to offer a training session that provides a general overview of both *Steps* and the concept of biblical counseling. This training will also allow everyone to learn from one another's experiences and will allow new members and leaders to ask questions and learn from those who have previously completed *Steps.*

Disc 2 of the videos provided in *Steps Bible Study Kit* includes a brief segment titled "Mentors and the Assessment Process" that can be shown during this training.

This training session would be a good time to distribute leader guides and mentor guides. Be sure you have ordered member books to distribute to all participants at the first group session.

Group Guidelines

The following biblical principles help provide a safe, nurturing, and orderly environment for *Steps* groups as we pursue redemption in Christ. Group Leaders should regularly communicate these guidelines to group members throughout *Steps*.

SHARING

- Share with honesty and authenticity. Sharing our struggles with honesty and authenticity demonstrates our desire to pursue growth and freedom in Christ.
- Speak the truth in love. God uses His people as agents of change in the lives of others. If we offer counsel to others, we should do so in an honest yet humble way.
- Do not monopolize the group. Group leaders should encourage participants who may share excessively to allow other group members the opportunity to share.
- Do not romanticize your sin. We do not celebrate our sin; we celebrate repentance. It is tempting in a group setting to compare struggles or take pride in things that actually grieve the heart of God.

GOSSIP AND CONFIDENTIALITY

Do not gossip. Group leaders will address all instances of gossip.

Note: Though we do not offer confidentiality in the traditional therapeutic sense, we do not betray confidences. However, if necessary, we will move beyond the walls of the group to love and lead our people in the following instances.

- Potential harm to self or others
- Reports of abuse or potential abuse to a child, the disabled, or an elderly person
- Severe outward and unrepentant sin within our covenant community

CARING RELATIONSHIPS

Be intentional about developing relationships. Group leaders and group members alike should seek intentional opportunities to pursue relationships with group members outside the group. Gospel-centered community goes beyond group sessions alone.

GROUP DIRECTION

Let the leaders lead. Group gatherings (discussion, prayer, confession, etc.) should be led by recovery-group leaders in an orderly way. Leaders set the direction for a group as they shepherd group members.

QUESTIONS

Honest questions are encouraged but are not always addressed directly. If group members have a question, a leader may be able to address it during the session. If not, he or she will answer before or after the session.

BIBLICAL COUNSEL

Counsel must be biblically rooted. Counsel to others must be driven by biblical truths and God-oriented purposes. Counsel that leaders provide will be rooted in God's Word.

We are not a professional counseling center but a church. Our leaders, ministers, and pastors are serving as ministers of the gospel.

CONFESSION & PRAYER

Practice confession; ask for prayer. The evidence of repentance includes confession and prayer. Recovery groups exist as a form of community in which confession and prayer are modeled by leaders and group members. Be quick to confess and quick to request prayer.

Share evidence of God's grace. As we pursue Christ together, we celebrate the victories that God brings because of the gospel. Group leaders should encourage group members to share ways God is at work in their lives.

LOVING CONFRONTATION

Be willing to challenge participants in a healthy way. Group leaders should lovingly confront sin and provide encouragement toward faithfulness from God's Word.

Pursue group members on a heart level in order to bring about transformation and growth in Christlikeness. Address group members' love for God, demonstrated by the way they pursue him in their day-to-day lives.

1. Paul Tripp, "Advent: The Promise" [online], 12 December 2012 [cited 2 October 2015]. Available from the Internet: *www.paultripp.com/wednesdays-word/posts/advent-the-promise.*
2. Adapted from "Seven A's of Confession," *Peacemaker Ministries* [online], 22 September 2014 [cited 5 October 2015]. Available from the Internet: *http://peacemaker.net/project/seven-as-of-confession/.*

Group Commitment and Information

GROUP COMMITMENT

Record the hopes and desires of group members as they begin this process.

_____

_____

_____

_____

_____

_____

_____

_____

_____

_____

_____

Review the following note and statements. Ask everyone to check each box and sign and date their commitments. Explain that you are making the same commitment to them.

NOTE: _Steps_ is not just a personal commitment. Your commitment is to the entire group, including the other members, your leader, and your mentor.

- ☐ I commit to complete the personal study and assessments each week during _Steps_.
- ☐ I commit to being honest with myself, my group, my leader, my mentor, and God.
- ☐ I commit to being present for the group session each week.
- ☐ I commit to actively listening during the teaching and to participating in discussion.

_____

Signature   Date

GROUP INFORMATION

MEETING DAY AND TIME   LOCATION

GROUP MEMBERS AND CONTACT INFORMATION   MENTORS AND CONTACT INFORMATION

_____

_____

_____

_____

_____

_____

_____

_____

_____

_____

_____

_____

_____

_____

_____

_____

Beginning *Steps* Discipleship

BEFORE YOU MEET

PRAYERFULLY PREPARE

Pray for the people who will be joining the group. Ask the Holy Spirit to move them into a posture of humility and openness to God's work through *Steps*.

WHEN YOU MEET

MINISTRY—*Session Goal*

The goal of this session is to introduce each person to one another and to *Steps*.

■ PRAYER, ACCOUNTABILITY, & ADMINISTRATION—*10 Minutes*

Ask God to make this time fruitful for His kingdom and to lead the session through His Word and the Holy Spirit as you submit to Him. Begin the session with the following.

- Open in prayer.
- Read group guidelines.
- Explain the homework and distribute member books.
- Explain the mentor relationship. (Introduce mentors if they are present during this introductory group session)
- Record group information on the previous page.

Instruct group members to fill out the Information page with the meeting time and place and everyone's name and contact information.

NOTE: If some people are not comfortable sharing their contact information with the group at this point, request that they provide that information to you after the group session. It is important that you, as the group leader, are able to reach out to everyone in your group. This simple step builds a level of trust and accountability with each group member.

ASK & LISTEN—*40 Minutes*

Offer help: Communicate that if anyone has further questions about any part of the program, you are available to help after the session.

Questions: To begin establishing a sense of community, prompt discussion and ask questions to help participants get to know one another. For example:

1. Ask everyone to share their name and how they heard about *Steps*.
2. As a leader, share your testimony and how God used *Steps* in your own life.
3. Ask everyone to describe any past or present church involvement.
4. Ask whether anyone is willing to share any fears or concerns about the *Steps* process or about being in a group like this.
5. Ask everyone to share what they hope to get out of their experience in *Steps*.

NOTE: You may want to make note of members' answers as important reminders throughout this process and as important points of review.

Direct everyone's attention to the Group Commitment. Have each member record the goals they may or may not have shared with the group. Have everyone read and complete the Commitment section at the bottom of that page.

SPEAK & ENCOURAGE—*10 Minutes*

Use this time to encourage the group, assuring participants that you are for them. This week encourage participants by saying their presence speaks volumes about the value they are placing on their spiritual growth.

Exhort: Encourage the group to be faithful to do the work by meeting with their mentors and completing the homework for session 1. Encourage them not just to check these off their to-do lists but to really seek the Lord.

■ RESPOND—*5 Minutes*

Ideally, leave a few minutes at the end of each session for the group to interact as the Holy Spirit moves. This is an opportunity for members to share something the Spirit is impressing on them, like a confession, a word of encouragement, or a verse.

■ PRAY: COVER WITH THE GOSPEL—*5 Minutes*

As participants are transparent and bare their souls, it is important that we cover them with the gospel in prayer as we conclude.

■ TEACHING—*45–60 Minutes*

If your ministry has chosen to provide the video teaching before group members complete their personal study, watch video session 1 or transition to a time of teaching.

If your ministry has chosen to provide the video teaching after group members complete their personal study, transition to a time of corporate worship or dismiss.

AFTER YOU MEET

SHEPHERDING TASK

During the first two sessions it is important to begin getting to know your group members and establishing personal relationships. This builds a level of trust and vulnerability.

Shepherds know their sheep by name. Get to know participants' names and circumstances. Contact those who may not have shown up for the first session. Reach out to participants, pray with them, and ask whether they have any questions.

NOTES

_____

_____

_____

_____

_____

_____

_____

_____

REFLECTION—*Seeing Through God's Eyes*

A prayerful time of reflection will help lead you to speak redemptively into the lives of group members. This is an ideal time for discipleship as the leader pours into the apprentice leader(s) and then prays for participants.

PRAY FOR GROUP MEMBERS

Join with your apprentice(s) in asking the Lord to move in the hearts and lives of group members and watch for Him to move.

Ask the Lord to help you see each participant through His eyes and speak redemptively into their situation. The following questions are meant to guide you, but don't feel that you need to answer every question every week or let them limit ways the Lord might speak.

- Where is this person spiritually?
- What areas need healing?
- Were any lies spoken about the truths of God and His character?
- What sinful patterns or strongholds did you discern?
- How could you encourage this person?
- What Scriptures speak to their situation?

NOTES

CREATION AND FALL

Viewer Guide I

There is only one God, and He alone __*created*__ all things.

There's a response that God has to His creation: it was __*good*__.

God endows and bestows a __*dignity*__ and a __*worth*__ on this special part of creation known as man and woman.

In His authority God is establishing __*boundaries*__ and giving instructions for how humanity can flourish.

The Bible is laying forth a correct __*diagnosis*__ of what has gone awry in the world and in your heart and mine.

God created humanity for a purpose: to __*relate*__ to Him and __*enjoy*__ Him and __*glorify*__ Him forever.

You and I, since the fall, have been in a posture and a position of __*rebellion*__ and enmity against the true God.

What you and I have earned because of our sin, what we deserve because of sin, is __*death*__.

An eternal punishment is just because there's a holy and righteous God we have __*offended*__.

Sin is not simply __*what*__ you do. It's __*who*__ you are.

I am a child of __*wrath*__, and I have been since the beginning.

I need a __*rescuer*__.

To the beautiful, God says, "You're __*broken*__."

To the broken, God says He's in the business of __*re-creating*__.

Why Gospel-Centered Recovery?

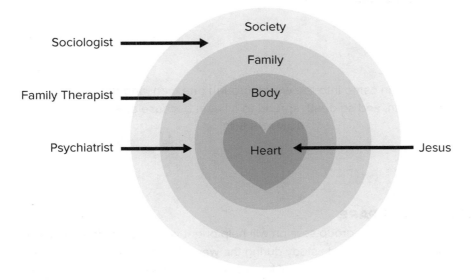

John Henderson, *Equipped to Counsel* (Bedford, TX: Association of Biblical Counselors, 2008).

NOTES

_____

_____

_____

_____

_____

_____

_____

_____

_____

_____

_____

Creation and Fall

Just as sin came into the world through one man, and death
through sin, and so death spread to all men because all sinned ...
ROMANS 5:12

BEFORE YOU MEET

PRAYERFULLY PREPARE

Taking time to plan for your group session will help orient your heart before the Lord
and understand what participants study during the week. Spend time in the Scriptures
and in the member book, making note of important truths. This way God's Word will be
fresh on your heart, providing the truth necessary to keep the session on track.

THIS WEEK'S SCRIPTURES

Day 1: *Genesis 1:1–2:3*

Day 2: *Genesis 2:4-25*

Day 3: *Genesis 2:18-25; Matthew 19:1-10; 1 Corinthians 7:10-11*

Day 4: *Genesis 3*

Day 5: *Genesis 3:7-24*

Day 6: *Genesis 4:1-16*

NOTES

_____

_____

_____

_____

_____

_____

_____

_____

GOING DEEPER—*To Be Discussed with Mentors*

Identify key questions to supplement the small-group discussion, if needed.

1. What do you think it means to fear the Lord?
2. Where does your heart go when you read the creation account?
3. Where does your heart go when you consider the suffering, pain, and hardship of our fallen world?
4. How does understanding God's pursuit and plan for redemption affect you?
5. According to the creation account, a functional human being is to live in a loving, dependent relationship with his Creator. In what areas of your life do you rely on creation rather than the Creator for direction, protection, provision, power, satisfaction, comfort, security, stability, hope, and happiness?
6. Describe your current suffering. What is the source?
7. God created us to be in loving relationships with Himself and others. Think about your close community and friends. Do you reach out to others when you need help? Why or why not? Where do they point you for hope?
8. In what ways do you disregard God's voice and follow another voice to pursue your own desires?
9. What do you do and where do you turn in your sin and suffering?
10. How do you attempt to remedy the problem? Or are you just defeated?

WEEK I SUMMARY

YOU HAVE HEARD IT SAID—*Wisdom of the World*

Traditional step 1: We admitted we were powerless over our addictions and compulsive behaviors—that our lives had become unmanageable.

GOD TELLS US IN HIS WORD—*Wisdom of God*

Redeemed truth from step 1: Man, in relationship to his Creator, has fallen from a place of dignity, humility, and dependence to a state of depravity, pride, and rebellion. This has led to unfathomable suffering. Any attempts on our own to redeem ourselves are futile, only increasing the problem of independence and self-sufficiency. Any perceived success leads only to empty vanity. Apart from Christ, we are powerless to overcome sin, and our attempts to control it only increase our chaos.

WHEN YOU MEET

MINISTRY—*Session Goal*

The goal of this session is to lead participants to realize that sin causes us to hide from God. Although we may hide in different ways, we have all hidden from God as a result of our sin.

■ PRAYER, ACCOUNTABILITY, & ADMINISTRATION—*10 Minutes*

Ask God to make this time fruitful for His kingdom and to lead the session through His Word and the Holy Spirit as you submit to Him. Begin each session with the following.

- Open in prayer.
- Read group guidelines.
- Ask whether participants completed their homework.
- Ask whether participants met with their mentors.
- Collect the attendance sheet.
- Collect participant agreements.

■ REVIEW, ASK, & LISTEN—*40 Minutes*

Offer help: Communicate that if anyone is struggling with any part of the program, you are available to help after the session.

Foster gospel-centered community through authenticity: We acknowledge the brokenness and suffering that have come into the world because of sin. We see our sin, but we see it in light of the transformative grace of Jesus. Share the importance of honesty and transparency. We welcome the weak, the wounded, the strayed, the lost, the addicted, and the abused who come honestly seeking help. Our group is a place where it is OK not to be OK. Adam and Eve were honest, while Cain covered his sin.

Questions: In keeping with God's pursuit of Adam in the garden, ask participants:

1. What was your biggest takeaway from your time in the Word and with your mentor this week?
2. Briefly describe the circumstances that have brought you to *Steps*.
3. How would you describe your relationship with God in the midst of these circumstances? Does it exist? Is it vibrant and fruitful or lacking? Are you confused, skeptical, struggling with doubt, hopeless, angry, afraid, or distrusting?
4. If needed, supplement the discussion with Going Deeper questions.

■ SPEAK & ENCOURAGE—*10 Minutes*

Use this time to encourage the group, assuring participants that you are for them. This week encourage participants by saying their presence speaks volumes about the value they are placing on their spiritual growth.

Speak redemptively: It is important for those we disciple to see their problems biblically so that we can bring the hope of the gospel to their specific needs. You might feel tempted to think you have to have all the answers immediately. eep your reflections for future sessions and for prayer. Introduce participants to Scriptures that speak to their circumstances. Remind them of their identity and of the promises and character of God.

Reintegrate: Emphasize the hope of the gospel from this session's teaching.

> **Genesis 3:15:** God's promise of a Redeemer was fulfilled in Jesus Christ.
> **Genesis 1:** God brings light to the darkness, life to our emptiness, and order to our chaos.

> **Redeemed truth from step 1:** Man, in relationship to his Creator, has fallen from a place of dignity, humility, and dependence to a state of depravity, pride, and rebellion. This has led to unfathomable suffering. Any attempts on our own to redeem ourselves are futile, only increasing the problem of independence and self-sufficiency. Any perceived success leads only to empty vanity. Apart from Christ, we are powerless to overcome sin, and our attempts to control it only increase our chaos.

Exhort: Encourage the group to be faithful to do the work by meeting with their mentors and completing the homework for session 1. Encourage them not just to these off their to-do lists but to really seek the Lord.

■ RESPOND—*5 Minutes*

Ideally, leave a few minutes at the end of each session for the group to interact as the Holy Spirit moves. This is an opportunity for members to share something the Spirit is impressing on them, like a confession, a word of encouragement, or a verse.

■ PRAY: COVER WITH THE GOSPEL—*5 Minutes*

As participants are transparent and bare their souls, it is important that we cover them with the gospel in prayer as we conclude.

■ TEACHING—*45–60 Minutes*
Watch the video or transition to a time of teaching.

AFTER YOU MEET

SHEPHERDING TASK

Shepherds know their sheep by name. Get to know participants' names and circumstances. Contact those who may not have shown up for the first session. Reach out to participants, pray with them, and ask whether they have any questions.

We are all under the care of the Good Shepherd, Jesus Christ, who is the foundation and cornerstone of our faith. Consider the following ways you can let your group know that your heart's desire is to represent Him and mirror His attributes as their shepherd leader, while acknowledging that you also need His grace.

- Dependence on the Holy Spirit for guidance
- Active pursuit of God's will

NOTES

_____

_____

_____

_____

_____

_____

_____

_____

_____

_____

_____

REFLECTION *Seeing Through God's Eyes*

A prayerful time of reflection will help lead you to speak redemptively into the lives of group members. This is an ideal time for discipleship as the leader pours into the apprentice leader(s) and then prays for participants.

PRAY FOR GROUP MEMBERS

Join with your apprentice(s) in asking the Lord to move in the hearts and lives of group members and watch for Him to move.

Ask the Lord to help you see each participant through His eyes and speak redemptively into their situation. The following questions are meant to guide you, but don't feel that you need to answer every question every week or let them limit ways the Lord might speak.

- Where is this person spiritually?
- What areas need healing?
- Were any lies spoken about the truths of God and His character?
- What sinful patterns or strongholds did you discern?
- How could you encourage this person?
- What Scriptures speak to their situation?

NOTES

_____

_____

_____

_____

_____

_____

_____

_____

_____

_____

_____

NOTES

_____

_____

_____

_____

_____

_____

_____

_____

_____

_____

_____

_____

_____

_____

_____

_____

_____

_____

_____

_____

_____

THE REMEDY: THE GOSPEL

Viewer Guide 2

COMPLETE THIS VIEWER GUIDE AS YOU WATCH THE VIDEO FOR SESSION 2.

The world will come in and offer a false solution, a false hope, a false _gospel_.

Redemption: the _freedom_ purchased through a ransom, paid by a redeemer on behalf of the enslaved

There was an amount that we owed because of being enslaved to sin. Jesus, on the cross, paid the price for our freedom and _redeemed_ us.

The Enemy works through the world to entice the flesh, and it reveals that the brokenness is coming from our own _hearts_.

In the insanity of running to created things, we are looking to a physical thing to solve a _spiritual_ problem.

Whatever is in that seat of highest worship in our life, we will _pursue_ and _sacrifice_ for it.

We can just as easily trade in unrighteousness for self-righteousness when what we really need is _Christ's_ righteousness.

Jesus reaches into the cycle; interrupts the cycle; and offers a real solution, the true _gospel_ solution.

The offer of redemption is to be set free, not to rule your own life but redemption by way of getting a better _Master_ —Jesus.

The Insanity Cycle of Sin

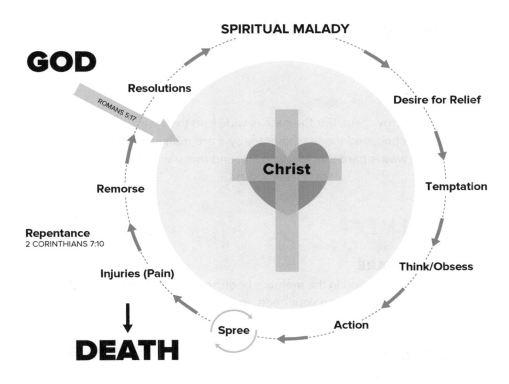

SPIRITUAL MALADY

GOD

Resolutions

ROMANS 5:17

Desire for Relief

Christ

Remorse

Temptation

Repentance
2 CORINTHIANS 7:10

Think/Obsess

Injuries (Pain)

Spree

Action

DEATH

NOTES

_____
_____
_____
_____
_____
_____
_____
_____
_____
_____
_____

The Remedy: The Gospel

Enter by the narrow gate. For the gate is wide and the way is easy that leads to destruction, and those who enter by it are many. For the gate is narrow and the way is hard that leads to life, and those who find it are few.
MATTHEW 7:13-14

BEFORE YOU MEET

PRAYERFULLY PREPARE

Spend time in the Scriptures and in the member book, making note of important truths. This way God's Word will be fresh on your heart, providing the truth necessary to keep the session on track.

THIS WEEK'S SCRIPTURES

Day 1: *Deuteronomy 5:1-22; Romans 3:20; Matthew 5:17-48*

Day 2: *Genesis 6:5-22; Exodus 11:1–12:13; Romans 1:18–2:3*

Day 3: *Isaiah 52:13–53:12; Isaiah 54–55*

Day 4: *John 1:1-14*

Day 5: *John 8:3-12*

Day 6: *Acts 17:16-34*

NOTES

_____

_____

_____

_____

_____

GOING DEEPER—*To Be Discussed with Mentors*
Identify key questions to supplement the small-group discussion, if needed.

1. In what ways do you suppress the truth or live in denial (see Rom. 1:18)?
2. Do you find yourself acting like a rebellious lawbreaker or a self-righteous Pharisee? How does that tendency express itself in your life?
3. If the antidote to unrighteousness is not self-righteousness, what is it?
4. What about Christ and the gospel did you find beautiful this week?
5. To what or to whom did you look for hope and love in the past? In what or in whom did you place your trust?
6. How did Paul clarify what the Athenians worshiped as "the unknown god" (Acts 17:23)? What might be the dangers of a vague spirituality?
7. Scripture is clear: we must make a decision about our belief in Jesus. What hangs in the balance if we do nothing?
8. How have you responded to the invitation to trust in the Suffering Servant?
9. If you believe in Christ, describe how you came to believe.

WEEK 2 SUMMARY

YOU HAVE HEARD IT SAID—*Wisdom of the World*
Traditional step 2: We came to believe that a power greater than ourselves could restore us to sanity.

GOD TELLS US IN HIS WORD—*Wisdom of God*
Redeemed truth from step 2: God lovingly intervened into our chaos and provided a remedy for the insanity of sin and the way back into fellowship with Him. We believe that by grace through faith in Jesus Christ, we can be redeemed.

WHEN YOU MEET

MINISTRY—*Session Goal*

The goal of this session is to lead participants to confess how they have searched for redemption apart from Jesus Christ and to explain why Jesus is better than their efforts.

■ **PRAYER, ACCOUNTABILITY, & ADMINISTRATION**—*10 Minutes*

Begin the session with the following.

- Open in prayer.
- Ask whether participants completed their homework.
- Ask whether participants met with their mentors.
- Collect the attendance sheet.

■ **REVIEW, ASK, & LISTEN**—*40 Minutes*

Offer help: Communicate that if anyone is struggling with any part of the program, you are available to help after the session.

Foster gospel-centered community through sound doctrine: The wisdom of God stands in stark contrast to the wisdom of world. The wisdom of God is meant to lead us to freedom, hope, and life. The wisdom of world will mislead us. Jesus Christ is the wisdom of God and the power of God. He is our message; therefore, we will guard our doctrine and lovingly confront lies.

Questions: Today we want to show how the gospel is superior to all the world offers in terms of redemption, rescue, and relief. Ask participants:

1. How does the culture define *redemption?* How could that definition apply to your current circumstances?
2. How does the Bible define *redemption?* How does the gospel bring redemption in a way that is superior to what the world offers?
3. When you are irritable, restless, and discontented, where have you sought redemption, rescue, and relief apart from the gospel? (Give examples from your life.)
4. If needed, supplement the discussion with Going Deeper questions.

- **Redemption** is freedom purchased through a ransom paid by a redeemer on behalf of the enslaved. Christ purchased our freedom from the bondage of sin by giving His life as a ransom.

- **The gospel** is the historical narrative of the triune God's orchestrating the reconciliation and redemption of a broken creation and fallen creatures from Satan, sin, and its effects to the Father and one another through the life, death, resurrection, and future return of the Son by the power of the Spirit for God's glory and the church's joy.
- **These symptoms (irritability, restlessness, and discontentment)** reflect a deeper problem of the heart, namely sin. The gospel provides intervention that is superior to all the world can offer (shopping, drinking, relationships, etc.).

■ SPEAK & ENCOURAGE—*10 Minutes*

Use this time to encourage the group, assuring participants that you are for them.

Speak redemptively: Use your reflections from prior sessions and prayer to take participants to Scriptures that speak to their circumstances. Remind them of their identity and of the promises and character of God.

Reintegrate: Emphasize the hope of the gospel from this session's teaching.

> **Genesis 3:15:** God's promise of a Redeemer was fulfilled in Jesus Christ.
> **Genesis 1:** He brings with him light to the darkness, life to our emptiness and order to our chaos.
>
> **Redeemed truth from step 2:** God lovingly intervened into our chaos and provided a remedy for the insanity of sin and the way back into fellowship with Him. We believe that by grace through faith in Jesus Christ, we can be redeemed.

Exhort: Encourage the group to be faithful to do the work by meeting with their mentors and completing the homework for session 2. Encourage them not just to check these off their to-do lists but to really seek the Lord.

■ RESPOND—*5 Minutes*

This is an opportunity for members to share something the Spirit is impressing on them, like a confession, a word of encouragement, or a verse.

■ PRAY: COVER WITH THE GOSPEL—*5 Minutes*

As participants are transparent and bare their souls, it is important that we cover them with the gospel in prayer as we conclude.

■ TEACHING—*45–60 Minutes*

Watch the video or transition to a time of teaching.

AFTER YOU MEET

SHEPHERDING TASK

Reach out to the mentors and check in with them. Pray with them for participants. Remind them of their importance as mentors and ask whether they have any questions.

NOTES

_____

_____

_____

_____

_____

_____

_____

_____

_____

_____

_____

_____

_____

_____

_____

_____

_____

_____

REFLECTION—*Seeing Through God's Eyes*

A prayerful time of reflection will help lead you to speak redemptively into the lives of group members. This is an ideal time for discipleship as the leader pours into the apprentice leader(s) and then prays for participants.

PRAY FOR GROUP MEMBERS

Ask the Lord to help you see each participant through His eyes and speak redemptively into their situation. The following questions are meant to guide you, but don't feel that you need to answer every question every week or let them limit ways the Lord might speak.

- Where is this person spiritually?
- What areas need healing?
- Were any lies spoken about the truths of God and His character?
- What sinful patterns or strongholds did you discern?
- How could you encourage this person?
- What Scriptures speak to their situation?

NOTES

_____

_____

_____

_____

_____

_____

_____

_____

_____

_____

_____

_____

_____

NOTES

THE RESPONSE: REPENTANCE

Viewer Guide 3

COMPLETE THIS VIEWER GUIDE AS YOU WATCH THE VIDEO FOR SESSION 3.

We have treated the gospel cheaply, while the gospel is actually __costly__. We have treated grace cheaply when grace is __great__.

The gospel—the good news—is that God did not leave us in that state but rather did act, did __intervene__. And His intervention was in His Son, Jesus Christ.

The good news is that in the offering of Jesus Christ—life that was righteous, sacrificed for our sake—we are __purified__ by grace through faith.

You cannot love __sin__ and love God.

God has commanded all of us, in light of our sin, to __repent__. It means literally to turn around.

Grace is not permission to run after things and not worry about ramifications or consequences, but rather, grace is a call out of those things to __repent__ and to __change__.

Our gratitude is contingent on the __greatness__ of the gift we've received.

We __war__ against temptation in repentance.

God has not provided you as the escape. God has provided __Himself__.

GAMES WE PLAY WHEN FACED WITH SIN
1. We __avoid__ the sorrow.
2. We __cover__ it up.
3. We run to __penance__.
4. We make __excuses__.

Repentance starts with understanding that God __knows__ and I don't, that God is __infinite__ and I am finite.

GODLY REPENTANCE	WORLDLY SORROW
VERTICAL	HORIZONTAL
FOCUSED ON GOD & OTHERS	FOCUSED ON SELF
SPIRITUAL	EMOTIONAL
WILLING	DEMANDING
ACTIVE	PASSIVE
HOPEFUL	HOPELESS
GRATEFUL	BEGRUDGING
PERSEVERING	TEMPORARY
HUMBLE	PRIDEFUL

NOTES

_____

_____

_____

_____

_____

_____

_____

_____

_____

_____

The Response: Repentance

Jesus came into Galilee, proclaiming the gospel of God,
and saying, "The time is fulfilled, and the kingdom
of God is at hand; repent and believe in the gospel."
MARK 1:14-15

BEFORE YOU MEET

PRAYERFULLY PREPARE

Spend time in the Scriptures and in the member book, making note of important truths. This way God's Word will be fresh on your heart, providing the truth necessary to keep the session on track.

THIS WEEK'S SCRIPTURES

Day 1: *James 2:14-26*
Day 2: *Isaiah 6*
Day 3: *John 3:16-21*
Day 4: *Luke 15*
Day 5: *John 14:15-31*
Day 6: *2 Corinthians 3:1–4:6*

NOTES

_____

_____

_____

_____

_____

_____

_____

GOING DEEPER—*To Be Discussed with Mentors*
Identify key questions to supplement the small-group discussion, if needed.

1. If you have received the gift of faith, how has that led to a heartfelt desire to obey God?
2. Describe any experiences in which God's presence and power humbled you.
3. Describe ways the reality of God's love has affected your life.
4. Describe how you view God. What do you believe about His character, attributes, attitudes, and motivations?
5. What is your attitude toward God?
6. What is your view of humankind?
7. Define *repentance*. What has been your response to the call to repent? Why?
8. What evidence of spiritual rebirth do you see in your life?
9. Have you surrendered your life to Christ? If so, describe the process. If not, why?

WEEK 3 SUMMARY

YOU HAVE HEARD IT SAID—*Wisdom of the World*
Traditional step 3: We made a decision to turn our will and our lives over to the care of God, as you understand Him.

GOD TELLS US IN HIS WORD—*Wisdom of God*
Redeemed truth from step 3: Through the Holy Spirit's illumination of our desperate and helpless condition before God and from the hope that comes through the gospel of Jesus Christ, we step out in faith and repent as an act of worship and obedience, surrendering our will and entrusting our lives to Christ's care and control. We are reborn spiritually and rescued from the domain of darkness and brought into the kingdom of light, where we now live as a part of Christ's ever-advancing kingdom.

WHEN YOU MEET

MINISTRY—*Session Goal*

The goal of this session is to lead participants to confess the evidence for faith and repentance in their lives. Evidence is not simply emotive in nature but rather contains a person's action, which might include confession, obedience, gratitude, worship, a submissive spirit, and surrender.

■ **PRAYER, ACCOUNTABILITY, & ADMINISTRATION**—*10 Minutes*

Begin session with the following.

- Open in prayer.
- Remind everyone of group guidelines, if necessary.
- Ask whether participants completed their homework.
- Ask whether participants met with their mentors.
- Collect the attendance sheet.

■ **ASK, LISTEN, & REVIEW**—*40 Minutes*

Offer help: Communicate that if anyone is struggling with any part of the program, you are available to help after the session.

Foster gospel-centered community through faith: Against competing redemptive schemes (self-help, false religion) we place our hope in a Redeemer, the resurrected Jesus Christ. It is only through faith in His life, death, and resurrection that we can be saved from our sin and become heirs to the promise of eternal life. This faith is not dead but causes us to repent and act according to God's redemptive purposes.

Questions: Many of us have had an inadequate or incomplete understanding of what it means to be covered by the gospel. Jesus arrived on the scene and proclaimed, "The time is fulfilled, and the kingdom of God is at hand; repent and believe in the gospel" (Mark 1:15). Ask participants:

1. How do you attempt to justify yourself before God and others?
2. What evidence can you point to from your life as to whether you have responded to the gospel in faith?
3. If needed, supplement the discussion with Going Deeper questions.

■ SPEAK & ENCOURAGE—*10 Minutes*

Use this time to encourage the group, assuring participants that you are for them.

Speak redemptively: Use your reflections from prior sessions and prayer to take participants to Scriptures that speak to their circumstances. Remind them of their identity and of the promises and character of God.

Reintegrate: Emphasize the hope of the gospel from this session's teaching.

> **Luke 15:** Whether we are self-righteous conformists or rebellious lawbreakers, our Heavenly Father beckons His children to repent and enjoy the blessing of living under his authority.

> **Redeemed truth from step 3:** Through the Holy Spirit's illumination of our desperate and helpless condition before God and from the hope that comes through the gospel of Jesus Christ, we step out in faith and repent as an act of worship and obedience, surrendering our will and entrusting our lives to Christ's care and control. We are reborn spiritually and rescued from the domain of darkness and brought into the kingdom of light, where we now live as a part of Christ's ever-advancing kingdom.

Exhort: Encourage the group to be faithful to do the work by meeting with their mentors and completing the homework for session 3. Encourage them not just to check these off their to-do lists but to really seek the Lord.

■ RESPOND—*5 Minutes*

This is an opportunity for members to share something the Spirit is impressing on them, like a confession, a word of encouragement, or a verse.

■ PRAY: COVER WITH THE GOSPEL—*5 Minutes*

As participants are transparent and bare their souls, it is important that we cover them with the gospel in prayer as we conclude.

■ TEACHING—*45–60 Minutes*

Watch the video or transition to a time of teaching.

AFTER YOU MEET

SHEPHERDING TASK

Follow up with group members who are not actively participating in the group sessions. Schedule one-on-one time with them and continue to pray for them.

NOTES

_____

_____

_____

_____

_____

_____

_____

_____

_____

_____

_____

_____

_____

_____

_____

_____

_____

_____

_____

_____

_____

REFLECTION—*Seeing Through God's Eyes*

A prayerful time of reflection will help lead you to speak redemptively into the lives of group members. This is an ideal time for discipleship as the leader pours into the apprentice leader(s) and then prays for participants.

PRAY FOR GROUP MEMBERS

Ask the Lord to help you see each participant through His eyes and speak redemptively into their situation. The following questions are meant to guide you, but don't feel that you need to answer every question every week or let them limit ways the Lord might speak.

- Where is this person spiritually?
- What areas need healing?
- Were any lies spoken about the truths of God and His character?
- What sinful patterns or strongholds did you discern?
- How could you encourage this person?
- What Scriptures speak to their situation?

NOTES

_____

_____

_____

_____

_____

_____

_____

_____

_____

_____

_____

_____

_____

_____

NOTES

THE RESULT:
JUSTIFICATION, ADOPTION, AND SANCTIFICATION

Viewer Guide 4

COMPLETE THIS VIEWER GUIDE AS YOU WATCH THE VIDEO FOR SESSION 4.

What makes you a member of the kingdom of God is not the right things you do but the __acceptance__ you receive.

Rebirth or regeneration: the Spirit's work of making us __new__

Conversion: the act of the regenerated person to __believe__, to __trust__, to __repent__, to place __faith__ in the work and the power of God

Justification: declaring __innocence__

Adoption: God declares us to be __sons__ and __daughters__.

Sanctification: The Holy Spirit is empowering us, but we are __participating__ in God's work to mature and to grow and to sanctify us.

It's your __heart__ that must be affected and changed for your joy. It's your heart that must __change__ to fight those sin issues.

The Spirit of God is regenerating, is repairing, is fixing the __brokenness__ of our hearts.

Glorification: We are already forgiven and already accepted and already declared innocent. There is this __future__ __hope__ of that fully being realized.

We have to know that under the covering of His grace, we can pursue honesty and transparency and openness about the ways we've __sinned__ against God and others.

Those that are reborn into the kingdom of God cannot be __unborn__.

This process of sanctification can be __painful__.

Sanctification is not all __you__.

What He's providing in His Spirit is exactly what we __need__ to navigate this sanctification process.

Salvation

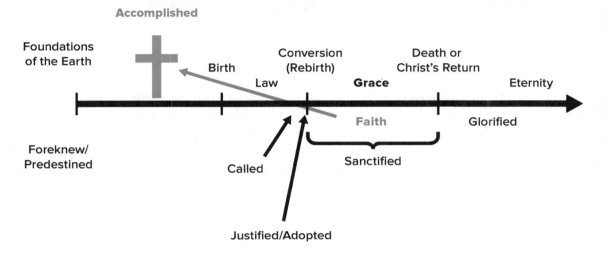

A Biblical Anthropology of the Active and the Passive Heart

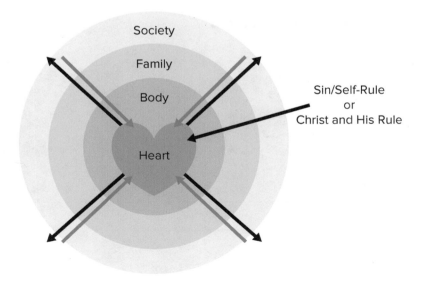

John Henderson, *Equipped to Counsel* (Bedford, TX: Association of Biblical Counselors, 2008).

THE RESULT: JUSTIFICATION, ADOPTION, AND SANCTIFICATION

Those whom he foreknew he also predestined to be conformed to the image of his Son, in order that he might be the firstborn among many brothers. And those whom he predestined he also called, and those whom he called he also justified, and those whom he justified he also glorified.

ROMANS 8:29-30

BEFORE YOU MEET

PRAYERFULLY PREPARE

Spend time in the Scriptures and in the member book, making note of important truths. This way God's Word will be fresh on your heart, providing the truth necessary to keep the session on track.

THIS WEEK'S SCRIPTURES

Day 1: *Romans 8*
Day 2: *Romans 6*
Day 3: *Matthew 15:1-20*
Day 4: *Revelation 21–22*
Day 5: *Ephesians 4:17–5:2*
Day 6: *Galatians 2:15–3:3*

NOTES

_____

_____

_____

_____

_____

GOING DEEPER—*To Be Discussed with Mentors*

Identify key questions to supplement the small-group discussion, if needed.

1. How do you tend to view suffering? How have the precious truths of Romans 8 shaped your views?
2. Paul rebuked the church in Galatia for trying to perfect themselves through human effort alone (works). How have you tried to overcome sin by trying harder instead of trusting the Holy Spirit's work in you (grace)? Explain the difference.
3. In what ways have you made excuses or placed blame for your ungodly thoughts, behaviors, and emotions (examples: family upbringing, suffering or loss, a medical or psychological diagnosis, "the Devil made me do it," blaming others)?
4. What grievous ways has God revealed to you?
5. Instead of presenting yourself for unrighteousness, how can you use the same effort, enthusiasm, and creativity to present yourself to God as an instrument of righteousness (see Rom. 6:13)?
6. What evidence of the Spirit of God do you see working in you?
7. What are your thoughts, concerns, and fears about completing your assessment?
8. What time will you set aside to complete your assessment? When will you meet with your mentor to share your assessment?
9. Why is it important to keep the gospel in full view as you dig into the dark places of your heart?

WEEK 4 SUMMARY

YOU HAVE HEARD IT SAID—*Wisdom of the World*

Traditional step 4: We made a searching and fearless moral assessment of ourselves.

GOD TELLS US IN HIS WORD—*Wisdom of God*

Redeemed truth from step 4: As children of God armed with the Holy Spirit and standing firm in the gospel, we engage in the spiritual battle over the reign and rule of our hearts. God set us apart for holiness, and we look to put to death the areas of our lives that keep us from reflecting Jesus Christ to a dark and dying world. We first examine the fruit in our lives (or moral symptoms). As we move through the assessment process, we will uncover the roots of any ungodly fruit (pride and idolatry) that drive our ungodly thoughts, actions, and emotions.

YOU HAVE HEARD IT SAID—*Wisdom of the World*
Traditional step 5: We admitted before God, ourselves, and another human being the exact nature of our wrongs.

GOD TELLS US IN HIS WORD—*Wisdom of God*
Redeemed truth from step 5: Under the covering of God's grace, we step out in faith, leaving behind our old, self-protective ways of covering sin and hiding from God. We prayerfully come into the light, confessing our sins before God and to one another so that we may be healed.

WHEN YOU MEET

MINISTRY—*Session Goal*
The goal of this session is to lead participants to confess the truths of the gospel with their mouths, while acknowledging areas where more faith is needed as they begin to complete their assessments.

Next week we will begin with the Anger and Abuse assessment, putting our faith into action by bringing into the light what was once hidden so that we can be healed.

■ **PRAYER, ACCOUNTABILITY, & ADMINISTRATION**—*10 Minutes*
Begin the session with the following.

- Open in prayer.
- Remind everyone of group guidelines, if necessary.
- Ask whether participants completed their homework.
- Ask whether participants met with their mentors.
- Collect the attendance sheet.

■ **ASK, LISTEN, & REVIEW**—*40 Minutes*
Offer help: This next week we will begin our assessments. Each group member will need to intentionally set aside time to examine their hearts before the Lord (instead of completing daily devotionals) and to meet with their mentors (three consecutive hours each week are suggested). This week we will examine the often dark realities of resentment (unresolved anger) and abuse. Communicate that if anyone is struggling with any part of the program, you are available to help after the session.

Foster gospel-centered community by dealing radically with sin: Sin is not a pet we keep around to entertain us. We do not try to tame it, but instead, we put it to death. We do this by confessing and repenting of our sin. In Jesus, God has freed us from the dominion of sin. The Holy Spirit, who has taken up residence in our hearts, empowers us to flee the sin to which we were once enslaved. We fight sin by the power of God's grace, for His glory and our good.

Questions: This week we are introducing gospel truths (gospel indicatives) and gospel pursuits (gospel imperatives). It is fascinating to read your Bible with these lenses. For example, Ephesians 1–3 are filled with gospel indicatives that root believers in truth, while chapters 4–6 are filled with gospel imperatives, or commands, for what we are called to as believers. Ask participants:

1. What was your biggest takeaway from your time in the Word and with your mentor this week?
2. What are the unchanging truths of the gospel for believers?
3. What do you struggle to believe?
4. If needed, supplement the discussion with Going Deeper questions.

- Gospel truths are the unchanging realities for people who have been born again. They plant our lives in truth as we pursue the things the gospel calls us to.
- Gospel pursuits are what the gospel calls us to. They are commands. We pursue obedience to the things the gospel requires of us.

▮ SPEAK & ENCOURAGE—*10 Minutes*
Use this time to encourage the group, assuring participants that you are for them.

Speak redemptively: Use your reflections from prior sessions and prayer to take participants to Scriptures that speak to their circumstances. Remind them of their identity and of the promises and character of God.

Reintegrate: Emphasize the hope of the gospel from this session's teaching.

Romans 8: Regardless of good days or bad days, God is accomplishing the salvation of His people. There is no condemnation for those who are in Christ Jesus. Nothing can separate us from His love. We are His children. We are more than conquerors. We will be conformed to the image of His Son as we put to death the deeds of the flesh and set our minds on the Holy Spirit.

Redeemed truth from step 4: As children of God armed with the Holy Spirit and standing firm in the gospel, we engage in the spiritual battle over the reign and rule of our hearts. God set us apart for holiness, and we look to put to death the areas of our lives that keep us from reflecting Jesus Christ to a dark and dying world. We first examine the fruit in our lives (or moral symptoms). As we move through the assessment process, we will uncover the roots of any ungodly fruit (pride and idolatry) that drive our ungodly thoughts, actions, and emotions.

Redeemed truth from step 5: Under the covering of God's grace, we step out in faith, leaving behind our old, self-protective ways of covering sin and hiding from God. We prayerfully come into the light, confessing our sins before God and to one another so that we may be healed.

Exhort: Encourage the group to be faithful to do the work by meeting with their mentors and completing the homework for session 2. Encourage them not just to check these off their to-do lists but to really seek the Lord.

■ RESPOND—*5 Minutes*
This is an opportunity for members to share something the Spirit is impressing on them, like a confession, a word of encouragement, or a verse.

■ PRAY: COVER WITH THE GOSPEL—*5 Minutes*
As participants are transparent and bare their souls, it is important that we cover them with the gospel in prayer as we conclude.

■ TEACHING—*45–60 Minutes*
Watch the video or transition to a time of teaching.

AFTER YOU MEET

SHEPHERDING TASK

Begin to plan an event or two to gather for a less intensive time together, perhaps a meal at someone's house or dinner at a restaurant before a group session. Encourage participants to spend time daily in the Word and in prayer during the next three assessment weeks.

NOTES

REFLECTION—*Seeing Through God's Eyes*

A prayerful time of reflection will help lead you to speak redemptively into the lives of group members. This is an ideal time for discipleship as the leader pours into the apprentice leader(s) and then prays for participants.

PRAY FOR GROUP MEMBERS

Ask the Lord to help you see each participant through His eyes and speak redemptively into their situation. The following questions are meant to guide you, but don't feel that you need to answer every question every week or let them limit ways the Lord might speak.

- Where is this person spiritually?
- What areas need healing?
- Were any lies spoken about the truths of God and His character?
- What sinful patterns or strongholds did you discern?
- How could you encourage this person?
- What Scriptures speak to their situation?

NOTES

NOTES

_____

_____

_____

_____

_____

_____

_____

_____

_____

_____

_____

_____

_____

_____

_____

_____

_____

_____

_____

_____

_____

_____

_____

_____

ASSESSING ANGER AND ABUSE

Viewer Guide 5

COMPLETE THIS VIEWER GUIDE AS YOU WATCH THE VIDEO FOR SESSION 5.

Anger is righteous inasmuch as it captures God's __heart__ toward that which is producing the anger.

Unrighteous anger is when, out of pride, we react with anger to that which is interfering with our idolatrous desire and our __self-rule__.

REACTIONS TO UNRIGHTEOUS ANGER
1. We can __conceal__ it.   2. We can __unleash__ it.

If we are reacting unrighteously, that's a sign, a warning, an alarm that something or someone other than Jesus is __ruling__.

We are 100 percent __responsible__ for what comes out of us.

There is a day in the future when God, in His righteous anger, purely and perfectly will judge __unrighteousness__.

WHAT JESUS' VICTORY MEANS FOR THE ABUSED
1. Jesus __identifies__ with your pain.
2. Jesus made a way not only for you to be __healed__ from your abuse but also where He paid the __penalty__ for your sin that you might be made right with the Father.

HEART ISSUES OF THE ABUSED
1. A confusion of __responsibilities__   2. A confusion of __identity__

DISTORTED DESIRES
1. We can __dismiss__ God-given desires.
2. We can __elevate__ good desires to an unhealthy place.

LIES BEHIND A VICTIM MENTALITY
1. If this had not happened, I would be __OK__.
2. If God allowed this, then God is __bad__.
3. I'm the only one who can be __trusted__.

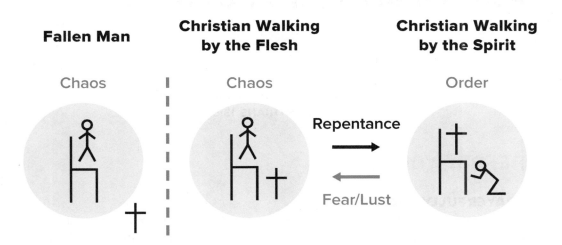

Adapted from Campus Crusade for Christ

NOTES

_____

_____

_____

_____

_____

_____

_____

_____

_____

_____

_____

WEEK 5

ASSESSING ANGER AND ABUSE

Examine yourselves, to see whether you are in the faith. Test yourselves.

2 CORINTHIANS 13:5

BEFORE YOU MEET

PRAYERFULLY PREPARE

These next three weeks will be formatted differently as group members enter the assessment process. Be sure you prepare to discuss anger and abuse. Taking time to prepare for the session will help orient your heart before the Lord and understand what group members have been working through during the week.

THIS WEEK'S SCRIPTURES RELATED TO ABUSE

Abuse is the misuse of anything. It is horrific. God created all things for His glory, and the misuse of His creation is abuse and ultimately sinful. All sin is abusive, and sin against the people it affects is undeserved. We will limit this assessment to attitudes and behaviors that are overtly abusive or have wounded your group members in a way that impairs their relationships with God and others.

The following Scriptures have been provided to group members to review before beginning their assessment. Take some time to review the verses.

Read: Matthew 15:1-14; Romans 6; 8; Galatians 2:15–3:3; Ephesians 4:17–5:2; Revelation 21–22.

NOTES

_____

_____

_____

_____

Jesus suffered abuse. He was neglected, betrayed, humiliated, stripped naked, beaten, and killed. His experience demonstrates three life-giving truths:

1. Jesus understands. He deeply understands what you have gone through and what you are feeling because He experienced it. He knows your pain.
2. Your abuse does not cause you to sin. Your response comes from the heart. Jesus did not respond to His abuse in sin or vengeance; He "continued entrusting himself to him who judges justly" (1 Pet. 2:23). The more Christ reigns and rules in your heart, the more Christlike your responses will be.
3. God will vindicate you and bring justice. For all those who do not repent, the wrath of God remains on them. And there will be justice.

GOING DEEPER—*Will Not Be Discussed with Mentors During Weeks 5–7*
During the assessment process group members will not review the Going Deeper questions together. Instead, this content is included in the When You Meet section for you to guide the small-group study and discussion.

A REDEMPTIVE VIEW OF ABUSE AND SUFFERING

BIBLICAL TRUTH
Psalm 56:1-11: This Scripture illustrates God's heart for the abused. He has not forgotten them; He has heard their cries. The cross of Christ not only justifies sinners but also vindicates victims.

Romans 8: God is saving us as victors despite the suffering we endure. We are no longer under His wrath and separated from His love. The Holy Spirit helps us in our weakness.

2 Samuel 13:13: Tamar, before being sexually violated by her brother, asked the question "As for me, where could I carry my shame?" Jesus is the answer to her question. He cares for us and covers our shame.

1 Peter 2:19-24: This Scripture explains that Jesus was also an abuse victim who suffered righteously and left us an example of how to respond to abuse. Through His wounds we are healed.

Genesis 16: This chapter shows how God redeemed a foreigner and sinner who had been mistreated by others and utilized her as a redemptive element in a hostile situation. She fled, but God saw, met her in her distress, called her by name, and spoke redemptively to her.

REDEEMED TRUTH ABOUT ABUSE

Abuse is the misuse of anything. God created all things for His glory, and the misuse of His creation is abuse and ultimately sinful. However, there is a type of abuse that moves beyond what might be considered normative in the Christian life. This abuse is horrifying and horrific, and in keeping with God's heart for the oppressed, the church must be a redemptive instrument in intervening and protecting. We cannot overcome sin independent of God. He has provided the way to overcome sin and its effects through the gospel of Jesus Christ. God does not allow abuse or any other form of suffering in the lives of His children without a redemptive purpose. In Christ, through the Holy Spirit, we can display His supremacy and victory over evil as we rise above sin, shame, and even death.

THIS WEEK'S SCRIPTURES RELATED TO RESENTMENT

The following Scriptures have been provided to group members to review before beginning their assessment. Take some time to review the verses.

Read: Luke 6:35-36; John 5:30; Romans 12:19; Hebrews 12:15

NOTES

_____

_____

_____

_____

_____

_____

_____

_____

GOING DEEPER—*Will Not Be Discussed with Mentors During Weeks 5–7*
During the assessment process group members will not review the Going Deeper questions together. Instead, this content is included in the When You Meet section for you to guide the small-group study and discussion.

A REDEMPTIVE VIEW OF ANGER AND RESENTMENT

BIBLICAL TRUTH
Psalm 4:4: Not all anger is sinful. We must go before the Lord to determine whether our anger is coming from selfish desires or agrees with the Holy Spirit's leadership to act in ways that push back darkness.

James 1:20: This verse reminds us that unrighteous anger is destructive and does not help to bring about a righteous end.

Mark 3:1-6: Jesus was angry in the synagogue because he was grieved at the hardness of men's hearts. His anger was motivated by a love for people and by anger toward sin. Notice that His anger moved Him to act in accordance with God's redemptive purposes.

Romans 12:19-21: We don't have to take revenge (or remain bitter), not because God doesn't care about justice but because He says He will bring perfect justice. He wants to take our burdens, and He cares.

Romans 2:1-5: God is righteous in His judgments, and apart from Him we are not. Outside the grace afforded to us through the gospel, we would deserve God's judgment. Many times when we have judged others, we place ourselves under God's judgment, showing that we are guilty of the same sins.

REDEEMED TRUTH ABOUT ANGER
Anger is an emotional response to a perceived wrong that demands justice. Not all anger is sinful; it can be the appropriate response to injustice. Unrighteous anger is rooted in man's attempts to meet his own idolatrous desires. Righteous anger is aligned with the Holy Spirit and flows from the heart of God in love for that which He cares about, spurring us on to gospel-centered action to eradicate evil and injustice.

WHEN YOU MEET

MINISTRY—*Session Goal*

The goal of this session is to lead participants to discuss what the Word of God says about anger and abuse. The session will follow a Bible-study format, but participants will not have prepared their answers beforehand because they were completing their assessments.

■ PRAYER, ACCOUNTABILITY, & ADMINISTRATION—*10 Minutes*

Begin the session with the following.

- Open in prayer.
- Remind everyone of group guidelines, if necessary.
- Ask whether participants completed their homework.
- Ask whether participants met with their mentors.
- Collect the attendance sheet.

■ ASK, LISTEN, & REVIEW—*40 Minutes*

Offer help: Communicate that if anyone is struggling with any part of the program, you are available to help after the session.

Foster gospel-centered community through confession: God's grace is the means and the motivation for us to bring our sin to light. When we confess our dead works before God and others, God brings healing to our lives. We confess sin in community so that we can continually submit our lives to God's loving care in a posture of humility and trust, knowing that forgiveness is ours in Jesus Christ. Because we have been united with Jesus Christ by faith, we have a new identity in Him.

Questions and Bible study: During the assessment process during weeks 5–7, this time will include focused Bible study related to anger and abuse. Ask participants the following questions.

1. When someone wrongs you, how do you typically respond? Give examples.

READ MATTHEW 5:21-22.

2. What is the point of Jesus' interpretation of the command not to murder?

READ ROMANS 12:9-21.

3. Most of us respond to evil by taking revenge. Such a response can take on many forms. Some people withhold love by withdrawing (becoming passive or suppressing our hurt. Others respond aggressively by yelling, throwing tantrums, or doing something worse. How are we commanded to respond to evil?

READ MATTHEW 5:38-42.

4. What examples did Jesus give for responding to personal offenses?
   • Point of interest: The response Jesus taught is not passive or aggressive but an act of generosity that allows the offender the opportunity to see his or her wrong.

READ MATTHEW 5:23-24.

5. What should we do if we remember that our brother has something against us?

READ JAMES 1:19-20.

6. What is man's anger unable to produce? Give examples of this truth in your life.

READ MATTHEW 18:15.

7. What are we to do if our brother sins against us?

READ EPHESIANS 4:26-27.

8. What wisdom should we take away from these verses? Based on today's discussion, what might the Lord be trying to tell you through His Word?

◼ SPEAK & ENCOURAGE—*10 Minutes*
Use this time to encourage the group, assuring participants that you are for them.

Speak redemptively: Use your reflections from prior sessions and prayer to take participants to Scriptures that speak to their circumstances. Remind them of their identity and of the promises and character of God.

Reintegrate: Emphasize the hope of the gospel from this session's teaching.

Our hope: God is reconciling the world to Himself through the work of Christ. He is righteous in His judgments and we can trust Him to forgive us when we confess our offenses. We were bought at a price. Jesus' sacrificial love frees us to be ambassadors of reconciliation to others.

Redeemed truth about abuse: Abuse is the misuse of anything. God created all things for His glory, and the misuse of His creation is abuse and ultimately sinful. However, there is a type of abuse that moves beyond what might be considered normative in the Christian life. This abuse is horrific, and in keeping with God's heart for the oppressed, the church must be a redemptive instrument in intervening and protecting. We cannot overcome sin independent of God. He has provided the way to overcome sin and its effects through the gospel of Jesus Christ. God does not allow abuse or any other form of suffering in the lives of His children without a redemptive purpose. In Christ, through the Holy Spirit, we can display His supremacy and victory over evil as we rise above sin, shame, and even death.

Redeemed truth about anger: Anger is an emotional response to a perceived wrong that demands justice. Not all anger is sinful; it can be the appropriate response to injustice. Unrighteous anger is rooted in man's attempts to meet his own idolatrous desires. Righteous anger is aligned with the Holy Spirit and flows from the heart of God in love for that which He cares about, spurring us on to gospel-centered action to eradicate evil and injustice.

Exhort: Encourage the group to be faithful to do the work by meeting with their mentors and completing the homework for session 5. Encourage them not just to check these off their to-do lists but to really seek the Lord.

■ RESPOND—*5 Minutes*
This is an opportunity for members to share something the Spirit is impressing on them, like a confession, a word of encouragement, or a verse.

■ PRAY: COVER WITH THE GOSPEL—*5 Minutes*
As participants are transparent and bare their souls, it is important that we cover them with the gospel in prayer as we conclude.

■ TEACHING—*45–60 Minutes*
Watch the video or transition to a time of teaching.

AFTER YOU MEET

SHEPHERDING TASK

> We urge you, brothers, admonish the idle, encourage
> the fainthearted, help the weak, be patient with them all.
>
> **1 THESSALONIANS 5:14**

As your group members continue in the assessment process, seek to model the characteristics of a loving shepherd found in 1 Thessalonians 5:14.

Whom do you need to admonish, encourage, help, and be patient with?

What action needs to flow from your role as a shepherd leader?

NOTES

_____

_____

_____

_____

_____

_____

_____

_____

_____

_____

_____

_____

_____

_____

_____

REFLECTION—*Seeing Through God's Eyes*

A prayerful time of reflection will help lead you to speak redemptively into the lives of group members. This is an ideal time for discipleship as the leader pours into the apprentice leader(s) and then prays for participants.

PRAY FOR GROUP MEMBERS

Ask the Lord to help you see each participant through His eyes and speak redemptively into their situation. The following questions are meant to guide you, but don't feel that you need to answer every question every week or let them limit ways the Lord might speak.

- Where is this person spiritually?
- What areas need healing?
- Were any lies spoken about the truths of God and His character?
- What sinful patterns or strongholds did you discern?
- How could you encourage this person?
- What Scriptures speak to their situation?

NOTES

ASSESSING SEX, GUILT, AND SHAME

Viewer Guide 6

COMPLETE THIS VIEWER GUIDE AS YOU WATCH THE VIDEO FOR SESSION 6.

When God created sex, He created it to be ___good___.

If the goal for sex is to have our own satisfactions met, then ultimately, it will become ___lust___.

Pornea: any form of ___sexual___ ___immorality___ that does not reflect God's intended desire

God does not offer intimacy to those He's not in ___covenant___ with.

The two should become one and never be ___separated___ again.

Real guilt: I have done something ___wrong___.

False guilt: I didn't do anything wrong, but I ___feel___ like I did something wrong.

Hard-heartedness: I did something wrong, and I should feel the weight of that, but I completely ___ignore___ it.

Shame: I'm defiled. I'm dirty. It's not that I did something wrong; it's that I ___am___ wrong.

Justification: I am guilty, but the Lord has declared me ___innocent___.

Adoption: Your identity has been conferred from being a simple and depraved man or woman to being a ___child___ of God.

When the Lord adopts us, we're no longer carrying the shame of that old identity. We've been made ___new___.

Sex is a beautiful and sacred gift given to us by God. It is to be worshipful but not ___worshiped___.

Two Heart Issues

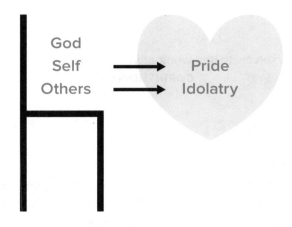

God
Self
Others → Pride
Idolatry

NOTES

_____

_____

_____

_____

_____

_____

_____

_____

_____

_____

ASSESSING SEX, GUILT, AND SHAME

Examine yourselves, to see whether you are in the faith. Test yourselves.
2 CORINTHIANS 13:5

BEFORE YOU MEET

PRAYERFULLY PREPARE

Be sure you prepare to discuss sex, guilt, and shame. Taking time to prepare for the session will help orient your heart before the Lord and understand what group members have been working through during the week.

THIS WEEK'S SCRIPTURES RELATED TO SEX

Sexual immorality is any sexual act that occurs outside God's intended design for sex between one man and one woman within the marriage covenant. Beyond sexual acts God looks deeper to the desires and motivations of the heart.

The following Scriptures have been provided to group members to review before beginning their assessment. Take some time to review the verses.

Read: Joel 2:25; Micah 7:18-20; 1 Corinthians 10:13-14; 1 John 3:2-3

NOTES

_____

_____

_____

_____

_____

_____

_____

A REDEMPTIVE VIEW OF SEX

BIBLICAL TRUTH

Psalm 56:1-11: This Scripture reveals that sex is God's idea. The Creator has a purpose for us, as His image bearers, in establishing His reign and rule on earth, filling the earth with His glory.

Genesis 2:18-25: The context for sex is within the confines of a heterosexual, monogamous marriage covenant before God.

Song of Solomon: This book celebrates sex as a good gift from God intended not only to have purpose but also to be enjoyed.

1 Corinthians 6:12-20: This Scripture indicates that Christ has purchased our redemption. As those indwelled by the Spirit of God, we do not engage in sexual immorality and defile the temple of the living God.

REDEEMED TRUTH ABOUT SEX

Sex is a beautiful, sacred gift given to us by God. It is to be worshipful but not worshiped. It is to be enjoyed and celebrated within the marriage covenant as a reflection of the gospel and our union with Christ. Any sexual act that occurs outside God's intended design is sexual immorality. Beyond action alone God looks deeper to the desires and motivations of the heart. Only through the gospel will God align our hearts with His purposes for this beautiful, sacred gift.

THIS WEEK'S SCRIPTURES RELATED TO GUILT AND SHAME

The following Scriptures have been provided to group members to review before beginning their assessment. Take some time to review the verses.

Read: Psalm 34:15-18,22; 71:1-3; John 1:7; Hebrews 4:15-16; 1 John 1:9

NOTES

_____

_____

_____

_____

A REDEMPTIVE VIEW OF GUILT AND SHAME

BIBLICAL TRUTH

Psalm 51:7: When Christ died on the cross, He took not only our sin but also our shame. In Him we are clean, pure, innocent, and white as snow.

Romans 8:1: This Scripture tells us, "There is therefore now no condemnation for those who are in Christ Jesus."

1 John 3:1-3: God has poured out His love for us in Christ, and now we are beloved children of God. A day is coming when we will be as He is.

Romans 5:1: Released from the demands of the law, we have been given right standing before God when He forgave our sins and imputed Christ's righteousness to us.

REDEEMED TRUTH ABOUT GUILT

Guilt can be both a state and a feeling that occurs when we have violated a law or a moral standard. We can feel guilty and not be guilty (false guilt), or we can be guilty and not feel guilty. False guilt occurs when someone besides God is the lord of our lives and their judgments matter more than His. Not feeling guilt when we are guilty is a sign of a hardened heart. Only the gospel can reconcile a heart of injustice. Life through the Holy Spirit brings conviction when we operate outside God's intended design.

REDEEMED TRUTH ABOUT SHAME

Shame is the intense feeling of being unclean, defiled, and dirty. Closely related to guilt, shame may result from the exposure of a person's own sin and depravity or from sin committed against a person's dignity. Shame is deeply rooted in identity ("I am worthless; I am dirty"). The gospel of Jesus Christ gives us a new identity and a covering for our shame. Even though we may sin or be sinned against, shame no longer rules our lives, because our identity is found in Jesus Christ.

WHEN YOU MEET

MINISTRY—*Session Goal*
The goal of this session is to lead participants to discuss what the Word of God says about sex, guilt, and shame. The session will follow a Bible-study format, but participants will not have prepared their answers beforehand because they were completing their assessments.

PRAYER, ACCOUNTABILITY, & ADMINISTRATION—*10 Minutes*
Begin the session with the following.

- Open in prayer.
- Remind everyone of group guidelines, if necessary.
- Ask whether participants completed their homework.
- Ask whether participants met with their mentors.
- Collect the attendance sheet.

ASK, LISTEN, & REVIEW—*40 Minutes*
Offer help: Communicate that if anyone is struggling with any part of the program, you are available to help after the session.

Foster gospel-centered community through prayer: God wants His church to be a people of prayer. God invites us into communion with him. Prayer allows our hearts to come in line with His and demonstrates our dependence on Him. During this study we have been praying a lot with our mentors.

Questions and Bible study: During the assessment process during weeks 5–7, this time will include focused Bible study related to anger and abuse. Ask participants the following questions.

1. What was your biggest struggle or takeaway in completing your assessment and meeting with your mentor this week?
2. How do you tend to view sex? Do you view it as dirty, delightful, gross, or a gift? Why?
3. According to Genesis 2 (life before the fall), who gives the gift of sex? What do you think the Giver intends for the gift?
4. Who owns and holds authority over sex? What context has God given for enjoying the gift?
5. Would past evidence support that you tend to despise the gift, worship the gift, or worship the Giver?

READ 1 CORINTHIANS 6:12-20.

6. What arguments about sexual immorality did the Corinthian church make, and how did Paul respond?
7. According to Paul, to whom are we to give ultimate glory with our bodies?
8. According to verse 18, what gospel imperative (command) did Paul use in dealing with sexual immorality?
9. In what gospel indicative (truth) did Paul root his command (see v. 19)?
10. What words describe the action of using a body for your own sexual pleasure against the owner's will?

READ MATTHEW 5:27-28.

11. Many people ask, "How far is too far?" in terms of sexual behavior. How did Jesus redirect the conversation away from outward appropriateness? In light of His teaching, how far is too far?

READ MATTHEW 5:20.

12. How is the gospel the only hope for a superior righteousness?
13. How can the sexual union of a man and a woman in marriage reflect the gospel or the relationship between Christ and His bride?
14. How can we apply gospel hope to those who have been defiled, either willingly or unwillingly, through sexual immorality?

SPEAK & ENCOURAGE—10 MINUTES

Use this time to encourage the group, assuring participants that you are for them.

Speak redemptively: Use your reflections from prior sessions and prayer to take participants to Scriptures that speak to their circumstances. Remind them of their identity and of the promises and character of God.

> **The character of God:** God is merciful. God does not give His children the punishment they deserve.
> **Our identity in Christ:** We are chosen by God, holy and dearly loved.
> **Gospel promise:** Our sins are forgiven—past, present, and future. We have received the righteousness of Christ.

Reintegrate: Emphasize the hope of the gospel from this session's teaching.

Psalm 51:7; 1 John 3:3: When Christ died on the cross, He took not only our sin but also our shame. In Him we are cleansed and purified, white as snow.

1 John 1:9: Use this verse to encourage participants. By bringing their sin into the light by faith, they can be forgiven of their sin and cleansed from the shame resulting from being defiled by others.

Redeemed truth about sex: Sex is a beautiful, sacred gift given to us by God. It is to be worshipful but not worshiped. It is to be enjoyed and celebrated within the marriage covenant as a reflection of the gospel and our union with Christ. Any sexual act that occurs outside God's intended design is sexual immorality. Beyond action alone God looks deeper to the desires and motivations of the heart. Only through the gospel will God align our hearts with His purposes for this beautiful, sacred gift.

Redeemed truth about guilt: Guilt can be both a state and a feeling that occurs when we have violated a law or a moral standard. We can feel guilty and not be guilty (false guilt), or we can be guilty and not feel guilty. False guilt occurs when someone besides God is the lord of our lives and their judgments matter more than His. Not feeling guilt when we are guilty is a sign of a hardened heart. Only the gospel can reconcile a heart of injustice. Life through the Holy Spirit brings conviction when we operate outside God's intended design.

Redeemed truth about shame: Shame is the intense feeling of being unclean, defiled, and dirty. Closely related to guilt, shame may result from the exposure of a person's own sin and depravity or from sin committed against a person's dignity. Shame is deeply rooted in identity ("I am worthless; I am dirty"). The gospel of Jesus Christ gives us a new identity and a covering for our shame. Even though we may sin or be sinned against, shame no longer rules our lives, because our identity is found in Jesus Christ.

Exhort: Encourage the group to be faithful to do the work by meeting with their mentors and completing the homework for session 6. Encourage them not just to check these off their to-do lists but to really seek the Lord.

■ **RESPOND**—*5 minutes*
This is an opportunity for members to share something the Spirit is impressing on them, like a confession, a word of encouragement, or a verse.

■ **PRAY: COVER WITH THE GOSPEL**—*5 minutes*
As participants are transparent and bare their souls, it is important that we cover them with the gospel in prayer as we conclude.

■ **TEACHING**—*45–60 minutes*
Watch the video or transition to a time of teaching.

AFTER YOU MEET

SHEPHERDING TASK
Reach out to mentors and check in with them about the assessment process. Pray with them and for their mentees. Remind them of upcoming mentor training and the night of worship.

NOTES

_____

_____

_____

_____

_____

_____

_____

_____

_____

REFLECTION—*Seeing Through God's Eyes*
A prayerful time of reflection will help lead you to speak redemptively into the lives of group members. This is an ideal time for discipleship as the leader pours into the apprentice leader(s) and then prays for participants.

PRAY FOR GROUP MEMBERS

Ask the Lord to help you see each participant through His eyes and speak redemptively into their situation. The following questions are meant to guide you, but don't feel that you need to answer every question every week or let them limit ways the Lord might speak.

- Where is this person spiritually?
- What areas need healing?
- Were any lies spoken about the truths of God and His character?
- What sinful patterns or strongholds did you discern?
- How could you encourage this person?
- What Scriptures speak to their situation?

NOTES

_____

_____

_____

_____

_____

_____

_____

_____

_____

_____

_____

_____

NOTES

ASSESSING FEAR, ANXIETY, AND GRIEF

Viewer Guide 7

COMPLETE THIS VIEWER GUIDE AS YOU WATCH THE VIDEO FOR SESSION 7.

Comfort: to come to someone's aid, to encourage, to come __*alongside*__ someone

Some suffering is as a result of our own __*sin*__. Some comes from being sinned against. And other suffering is just the tragic result of a __*fallen*__ world.

THREE TRUTHS ABOUT GOD
1. God __*loves*__ you.
2. God is __*good*__.
3. God is __*sovereign*__ and purposeful.

If you're under the covering of God's grace, there is literally nothing to __*fear*__.

Part of God's call on all of our lives is that we may be called at times to go places where we will experience suffering for His __*namesake*__.

You can't lose anything that's __*eternal*__, and you can't keep anything from here.

The two most primitive expressions of a prideful heart are __*lust*__ and __*fear*__.

Lusts seek to control and __*obtain*__. Fears seek to control and __*preserve*__.

We have our dependence not on us and our abilities to provide for ourselves but rather on the God who tells us He __*loves*__ us and who is __*sovereign*__.

If I am trusting in the Lord, nothing else can __*worry*__ me; nothing else can raise __*fear*__ in me.

STAGES OF GRIEF
1. __*Denial*__
2. __*Anger*__ and resentment
3. __*Bargaining*__
4. __*Depression*__ and alienation
5. __*Acceptance*__

A BIBLICAL UNDERSTANDING OF GRIEF

1. We move from denial to candor.
2. We move from anger to lament—getting honest with God.
3. We move from bargaining to crying out to God—asking God for help.
4. We move from depression and alienation to comfort—receiving God's help.
5. We move from regrouping and pushing forward in our own strength to waiting and trusting with faith when God says, "Not yet."
6. We move from deadening to wailing—groaning with hope.
7. We move from despairing and doubting to weaving—perceiving with grace.
8. We move from digging cisterns to worshiping God, the Redeemer.[1]

1. Adapted from Robert Kellemen, *God's Healing for Life's Losses* (Winona Lake, IN: BMH, 2010).

NOTES

_____

_____

_____

_____

_____

_____

_____

_____

_____

_____

_____

ASSESSING FEAR, ANXIETY, AND GRIEF

Examine yourselves, to see whether you are in the faith. Test yourselves.
2 CORINTHIANS 13:5

BEFORE YOU MEET

PRAYERFULLY PREPARE

This is the final week of personal assessments before returning to the personal Bible-study format. Be sure you are ready to discuss fear, grief, and anxiety. Taking time to prepare for the session will help orient your heart before the Lord and understand what group members have been working through during the week

THIS WEEK'S SCRIPTURES RELATED TO FEAR

Fear is an emotional response to a perceived threat or danger. Healthy fear prompts a person to act in the face of imminent danger. Fear is unhealthy when we feel afraid even though there is no imminent danger.

The following Scriptures have been provided to group members to review before beginning their assessment. Take some time to review the verses.

Read: Psalm 73:24-26; 91:9-16; 118:6; Philippians 4:5-6

NOTES

_____

_____

_____

_____

_____

_____

GOING DEEPER

Next week group members will resume completing daily homework and reviewing the Going Deeper questions with their mentors. In this session this content is included in the When You Meet section for you to guide the small-group study and discussion.

A REDEMPTIVE VIEW OF FEAR & ANXIETY

BIBLICAL TRUTH

1 Peter 3:6: The command not to fear does not mean there are not frightful things. God acknowledges the reality of frightening circumstances. However, we can trust that the love of God is more powerful than any danger we face.

1 John 4:7-21: The gospel of Jesus Christ removes the curse of sin and the wrath of God and allows us to approach His throne with confidence. Knowing His love for us frees us from self-protection and allows us to sacrificially lay down our lives so that others can know His love. When we walk in fear, we cannot walk in love.

Matthew 6:19-34: This passage teaches that our fears reveal our treasures or the things we covet. We fear not having the things we cannot live without. God offers us a reality beyond what is seen and transient that is secure.

Matthew 10:28: This passage suggests that our fear of God will displace our fear of lesser things. People can take from us only what is temporal and what we will eventually lose, but God offers something better that is eternal.

REDEEMED TRUTH ABOUT FEAR

Fear is an emotional response to a perceived threat or danger. Spiritually, healthy fear is the fear of the Lord. To fear the Lord is to worship Him alone and is the source of all wisdom and understanding. The absence of the fear of the Lord is the height of foolishness and leads to destruction. Outside the gospel we live our lives from a self-centered fear that seeks to meet our own perceived needs. As the Holy Spirit reveals this foolishness, we come under the compassion and care of our loving Father. He knows best in providing, protecting, and directing our lives according to His plan and purpose for His glory and our good.

THIS WEEK'S SCRIPTURES RELATED TO GRIEF

Grief is the deep sorrow over the loss of someone or something we love. This includes people, relationships, safety, security, identity, possessions, affections, and desires. Grief is a natural response to loss and is not sinful. Jesus wept at the tomb of Lazarus. We should grieve loss fully and in relationship with God. However, dealing with grief independently from God leaves us to cope rather than overcome. Coping leads to sinful patterns of dealing with loss.

Read: **Psalm 100; Isaiah 40:28-31; Ezekiel 37:1-6; John 6:49-51; 10:9-10; Colossians 3:1-2**

NOTES

_____

_____

_____

_____

_____

A REDEMPTIVE VIEW OF GRIEF

BIBLICAL TRUTH

Psalm 10:1; 22:1: Though it is sinful to stand in judgment of God, there is a way to confess your feelings of anger and frustration to God in an honest, humble manner. The psalmists were honest with God about feelings of anger, frustration, confusion, and abandonment.

Matthew 5:4: God comforts us as we cry out to Him.

Psalm 34:18-19: God is always present in our suffering. He promises to deliver us from our afflictions.

2 Corinthians 7:10: There is a type of grief that leads us away from God toward death, and there is a type of grief that leads us to God as He leads us through our sorrow.

REDEEMED TRUTH ABOUT GRIEF

Grief is a natural response to loss and is not sinful. When we grieve, we can do so knowing that we stand in the loving arms of God the Father. Grief in this context is always hopeful because we know that God is making all things new. Grief outside the gospel leaves us to cope through self-generated means and with false hope or no hope at all. Grief can become complicated when we idolize what we lost.

WHEN YOU MEET

MINISTRY—*Session Goal*

The goal of this session is to lead participants to discuss what the Word of God says about fear, anxiety, and grief. The session will follow a Bible-study format, but participants will not have prepared their answers beforehand because they were completing their assessments.

◼ PRAYER, ACCOUNTABILITY, & ADMINISTRATION—*10 Minutes*

Begin the session with the following.

- Open in prayer.
- Remind everyone of group guidelines, if necessary.
- Ask whether participants completed their homework.
- Ask whether participants met with their mentors.
- Collect the attendance sheet.

◼ ASK, LISTEN, & REVIEW—*40 minutes*

Offer help: Communicate that if anyone is struggling with any part of the program, you are available to help after the session.

Foster gospel-centered community through pursuing God: God pursues those He loves, and He calls us to pursue Him in joy. His love compels us to cast aside sinful patterns of relating to Him and others that are rooted in self-rule. As Christ becomes our treasure, we reflect Him in our loving pursuit of others.

Questions and Bible study: This is the final week to follow this format. We will have a focused time of Bible study related to fear, anxiety, and grief. Ask participants:

1. What was your biggest struggle or takeaway in working on your assessments and meeting with your mentors this week?
2. What makes you anxious? What do you worry about?

READ MATTHEW 6:19-34.

3. According to verse 19, what is easily threatened? How did Jesus instruct us, based on this reality?
   • Point of interest: There are two important concepts that we should be able to identify as we read the Scriptures: gospel truths and gospel pursuits. Gospel truths are facts that have already been accomplished in Christ. Gospel pursuits are imperative instructions (commands) that flow from life in Christ. Gospel truths (God's love and acceptance of us, sonship, etc.) should motivate our gospel pursuits (holiness, sanctification). Otherwise, we will stand on shaky ground and become insecure when we fall short. If we do not see the difference, we risk pursuing things that are already secure in Christ.
4. What gospel pursuit did Jesus give us in verse 20? In what gospel truth is this rooted (see v. 21)?
5. Why might our body be full of darkness if our eye is set on earthly treasures?
6. What does the location of our treasure reveal about our hearts?
7. What does Jesus' use of the word *masters* communicate about our treasure? What verbs did He use? What was Jesus saying about how many things can rule our hearts at once?
8. Jesus began verse 25 with the word *therefore,* connecting His words with the preceding verses. How is the symptom of anxiety connected to what we treasure?
9. What command did Jesus give in verse 25? In what gospel truth did He root this command (see vv. 26-27)?
10. How did Jesus appeal to reason in verse 27?
11. How did Jesus connect anxiety and unbelief? How does faith in the gospel help resolve anxiety?
12. What gospel pursuit did Jesus give in verse 33? In what gospel truths is it rooted?

■ SPEAK & ENCOURAGE—*10 minutes*
Use this time to encourage the group, assuring participants that you are for them.

Speak redemptively: Use your reflections from prior sessions and prayer to take participants to Scriptures that speak to their circumstances. Remind them of their identity and of the promises and character of God.

The character of God: God is compassionate. God sees, cares, and acts when His children are in need.

Our identity in Christ: As heirs to the kingdom, we are eternally secure.

Gospel promise: God will dwell with us and wipe away every tear. Death will no longer exist.

Reintegrate: Emphasize the hope of the gospel from this session's teaching.

Our hope: God is providential, meaning He is in control and acts in accordance with His character. God is good. God is love, so His actions always display love. God loves His children. As God's children, we know that our Father is mightier than any enemy.

"Fear not" is the most repeated command in the Bible. Though frightening circumstances are a reality, God is our loving, all-powerful Father who delights in caring for and protecting His children. He supplies all our needs and knows them before we ask. When we find ourselves in fear, we can instead focus our thoughts on the faithfulness of God. Our awe of Him displaces lesser fears.

Scripture reveals the hope of the gospel amid our loss. We can confess and cry out, "Abba! Father!" (Rom. 8:15) in our suffering, and God comforts us and promises to restore all that has been lost. There is nothing on earth that we can hold on to eternally, and there is nothing eternal that we can lose in Christ. We are secure in Him. Dealing with loss in sinful ways always brings captivity, but grief provides an opportunity to draw near to God and experience His presence so that we can know Him more intimately and experience the power of the resurrection.

> This light momentary affliction is preparing for us an eternal weight of glory beyond all comparison, as we look not to the things that are seen but to the things that are unseen. For the things that are seen are transient, but the things that are unseen are eternal.
> **2 CORINTHIANS 4:17-18**

Redeemed truth about fear: Fear is an emotional response to a perceived threat or danger. Spiritually, healthy fear is the fear of the Lord. To fear the Lord is to worship Him alone and is the source of all wisdom and understanding. The absence of the fear of the Lord is the height of foolishness and leads to destruction. Outside the gospel we live our lives from a self-centered fear that seeks to meet our own perceived needs. As the Holy Spirit reveals this foolishness, we come under the compassion and care of our loving Father. He knows best in providing, protecting, and directing our lives according to His plan and purpose for His glory and our good.

Redeemed truth about grief: Grief is a natural response to loss and is not sinful. When we grieve, we can do so knowing that we stand in the loving arms of God the Father. Grief in this context is always hopeful because we know that God is making all things new. Grief outside the gospel leaves us to cope through self-generated means and with false hope or no hope at all. Grief can become complicated when we idolize what we lost.

Exhort: Encourage the group to be faithful to do the work by meeting with their mentors and completing the homework for session 2. Encourage them not just to check these off their to-do lists but to really seek the Lord.

RESPOND—*5 minutes*
This is an opportunity for members to share something the Spirit is impressing on them, like a confession, a word of encouragement, or a verse.

PRAY: COVER WITH THE GOSPEL—*5 minutes*
As participants are transparent and bare their souls, it is important that we cover them with the gospel in prayer as we conclude.

TEACHING—*45–60 minutes*
Watch the video or transition to a time of teaching.

AFTER YOU MEET

SHEPHERDING TASK

Pursue those in your group who may need extra encouragement or direction. Consider whom you and your apprentice need to meet with individually.

NOTES

_____

_____

_____

_____

_____

_____

_____

_____

_____

_____

_____

_____

_____

REFLECTION—*Seeing Through God's Eyes*

A prayerful time of reflection will help lead you to speak redemptively into the lives of group members. This is an ideal time for discipleship as the leader pours into the apprentice leader(s) and then prays for participants.

PRAY FOR GROUP MEMBERS

Ask the Lord to help you see each participant through His eyes and speak redemptively into their situation. The following questions are meant to guide you, but don't feel that you need to answer every question every week or let them limit ways the Lord might speak.

- Where is this person spiritually?
- What areas need healing?
- Were any lies spoken about the truths of God and His character?
- What sinful patterns or strongholds did you discern?
- How could you encourage this person?
- What Scriptures speak to their situation?

NOTES

_____

_____

_____

_____

_____

_____

_____

_____

_____

_____

_____

_____

_____

_____

_____

_____

_____

_____

_____

GETTING TO THE ROOTS: OFFERING AND ASKING

Viewer Guide 8

Fruit in our life—good or bad—is really the outgrowth of what we __believe__, what we __treasure__, and what we give our __hearts__ to.

The original lie: You can go around God and not to God for __purpose__, for validation, and for meaning—for your life to be significant.

Spiritual adultery: giving the intimacy and worship that were created for __God__ to things and people

The Lord has given all of us good __desires__.

God does not want our desires to __own__ us, and He does not owe us the fulfillment of our desires on our own terms.

THREE ENEMIES
1. The __world__
2. The __flesh__
3. The __demonic__ realm

Satan wants to draw your attention away from God and to make you self-__absorbed__ just like he is.

Satan is always going to pounce on your __identity__.

Jesus shows us what it means to __trust__ __God__ when our desires are not being met.

God can break us by His grace from the curse of our self-absorption and the bad __fruit__ that's come with it.

The battle of your life is to continue to __renounce__ those old ways, to __uproot__ by His grace, and to __plant__ in the kingdom of God.

The Elevation of Desire

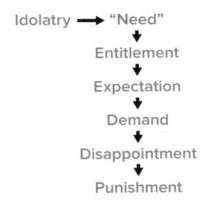

Idolatry ➡ "Need"
⬇
Entitlement
⬇
Expectation
⬇
Demand
⬇
Disappointment
⬇
Punishment

Adapted from Paul David Tripp, *War of Words: Getting to the Heart of Your
Communication Struggles* (Phillipsburg, NJ: P&R Publishing, 2000), 59.

Getting to the Roots of Ungodly Fruit and Character Defects

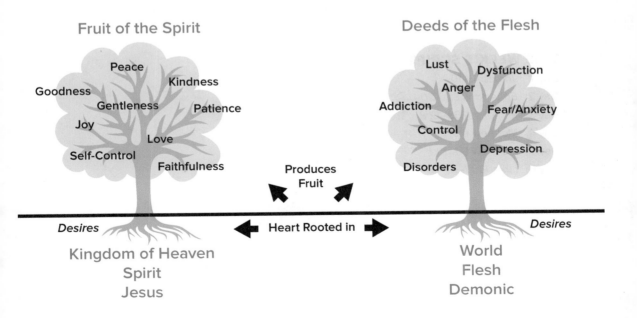

GETTING TO THE ROOTS: OFFERING AND ASKING

No good tree bears bad fruit, nor again does a bad tree bear good fruit, for each tree is known by its own fruit. For figs are not gathered from thornbushes, nor are grapes picked from a bramble bush. The good person out of the good treasure of his heart produces good, and the evil person out of his evil treasure produces evil, for out of the abundance of the heart his mouth speaks.

LUKE 6:43-45

BEFORE YOU MEET

PRAYERFULLY PREPARE

Spend time in the Scriptures and in the member book, making note of important truths. This way God's Word will be fresh on your heart, providing the truth necessary to keep the session on track.

THIS WEEK'S SCRIPTURES

Day 1: *James 4:1-10*
Day 2: *Ephesians 6:10-20*
Day 3: *Romans 11:33–12:8*
Day 4: *Matthew 6:9-13; 7:7-11*
Day 5: *Matthew 8:1–10:1*
Day 6: *Luke 18:18-30*

NOTES

_____

_____

_____

GOING DEEPER—*To Be Discussed with Mentors*
Identify key questions to supplement the small-group discussion, if needed.

1. Internal ruling desires lead to fights and quarrels. What desires tend to rule your heart and spark anger?
2. What do you turn to instead of God to fulfill your desires?
3. How do you attempt to satisfy your desire for peace?
4. Where do you typically look for hope?
5. Where do you find value, worth, and significance?
6. We all have an innate desire to belong to something bigger than ourselves. Historically, what lengths have you gone to in order to belong? Today what do you have in common with those who are closest to you?
7. To what lengths have you gone to meet your material needs? Have you ever sinned to meet those needs?
8. When we withhold an area of our lives from Christ and His lordship (authority), to whom do we give authority by default?
9. What character defects do you need to surrender to Jesus, trusting Him to provide the grace you need?
10. Are there areas of your life in which you still feel enslaved?
11. Are there physical, emotional, spiritual, or relational wounds that you desire Jesus to heal?
12. What gospel truths and gospel pursuits affected you most this week?

WEEK 8 SUMMARY

YOU HAVE HEARD IT SAID—*Wisdom of the World*
Traditional step 6: We are entirely ready to have God remove all these defects of character.
Traditional step 7: We humbly asked Him to remove our shortcomings.

GOD TELLS US IN HIS WORD—*Wisdom of God*
Redeemed truth from steps 6 & 7: In attempting to live independent of God, we have developed dysfunctional (sinful) patterns of coping. After careful examination we have begun to see the demonic roots of our slavery to these sinful patterns. We desire freedom. We renounce our former ways; offer ourselves to God; and, under the waterfall of His grace, ask Him to deliver and heal us by the authority of Christ and the power of the Holy Spirit. We also pray for blessing and the empowerment of the Holy Spirit to live life according to His kingdom purposes.

WHEN YOU MEET

MINISTRY—*Session Goal*

The goal of this session is to lead participants to confess ways they have sought to cope with sin apart from Jesus Christ and to identify ways the freedom found only in Jesus is better than their efforts.

■ **PRAYER, ACCOUNTABILITY, & ADMINISTRATION**—*10 Minutes*

Begin the session with the following.

- Open in prayer.
- Remind everyone of group guidelines, if necessary.
- Ask whether participants completed their homework.
- Ask whether participants met with their mentors.
- Collect the attendance sheet.

■ **ASK, LISTEN, & REVIEW**—*40 Minutes*

Offer help: Communicate that if anyone is struggling with any part of the program, you are available to help after the session.

Foster gospel-centered community through repentance: Repentance is the joy-filled process of submitting our lives fully to God's reign and rule of our hearts. We turn from sin and toward God as we put off the old man with its practices and put on the new man that is being shaped into the image of Christ.

Questions: We will now discuss the things the Lord is leading us to pray for as we move from considering the details of our assessment to renouncing our former ways as a community, asking Him to move mountains. Ask participants:

1. What character defects or sinful patterns of relating to God and others do you need to renounce and ask for deliverance?
2. What wounds (emotional, spiritual, or physical) need to be healed?
3. In what ways do you need to ask the Holy Spirit to empower you to live differently for His kingdom purposes?
4. If needed, supplement the discussion with Going Deeper questions.

■ **SPEAK & ENCOURAGE**—*10 Minutes*

Use this time to encourage the group, assuring participants that you are for them.

Speak redemptively: Use your reflections from prior sessions and prayer to take participants to Scriptures that speak to their circumstances. Remind them of their identity and of the promises and character of God.

Reintegrate: Emphasize the hope of the gospel from this session's teaching.

> **Matthew 6:19-34:** Life is so much more than the temporal world we see. We have been transferred from the dominion of darkness to the kingdom of the beloved Son. In this kingdom we find all our hearts desire.

> **Redeemed truth from steps 6 & 7:** In attempting to live independent of God, we have developed dysfunctional (sinful) patterns of coping. After careful examination we have begun to see the demonic roots of our slavery to these sinful patterns. We desire freedom. We renounce our former ways; offer ourselves to God; and, under the waterfall of His grace, ask Him to deliver and heal us by the authority of Christ and the power of the Holy Spirit. We also pray for blessing and the empowerment of the Holy Spirit to live life according to His kingdom purposes.

Exhort: Encourage the group to be faithful to do the work by meeting with their mentors and completing the homework for session 8. Encourage them not just to check these off their to-do lists but to really seek the Lord.

■ **RESPOND**—*5 Minutes*

This is an opportunity for members to share something the Spirit is impressing on them, like a confession, a word of encouragement, or a verse.

■ **PRAY: COVER WITH THE GOSPEL**—*5 Minutes*

As participants are transparent and bare their souls, it is important that we cover them with the gospel in prayer as we conclude.

■ **TEACHING**—*45–60 Minutes*

Watch the video or transition to a time of teaching.

AFTER YOU MEET

SHEPHERDING TASK

Plan a time to serve together as a group in the community or within the church. Also plan a final celebratory time to reflect on and remember the Lord's goodness and faithfulness during this experience.

NOTES

_____

_____

REFLECTION—*Seeing Through God's Eyes*

A prayerful time of reflection will help lead you to speak redemptively into the lives of group members. This is an ideal time for discipleship as the leader pours into the apprentice leader(s) and then prays for participants.

PRAY FOR GROUP MEMBERS

Ask the Lord to help you see each participant through His eyes and speak redemptively into their situation. The following questions are meant to guide you, but don't feel that you need to answer every question every week or let them limit ways the Lord might speak.

- Where is this person spiritually?
- What areas need healing?
- Were any lies spoken about the truths of God and His character?
- What sinful patterns or strongholds did you discern?
- How could you encourage this person?
- What Scriptures speak to their situation?

NOTES

_____

_____

_____

_____

_____

_____

PEACEMAKING, PART 1: RECONCILING AND AMENDING

Viewer Guide 9

COMPLETE THIS VIEWER GUIDE AS YOU WATCH THE VIDEO FOR SESSION 9.

The way we engage horizontally with others is informed by what takes place __vertically__.

In making amends, we have to make sure that we __see__ rightly.

Idols confuse, skew our vision to see rightly, and __estrange__ us from God.

What makes an idol bad is the way it provides comfort or peace or identity that is not derived from __God__.

If we don't see rightly, we'll never __confess__.

If we're known to God, we don't have to justify ourselves. We don't have to posture. We don't have to go in __fear__.

Every sin that you've committed—your history—is __redefined__ when Christ invades your life.

If you have sinned against someone, __confess__.

We confess, regardless of the __consequences__.

We go __forward__ with the aim to please Christ.

PRINCIPLES OF PEACEMAKING

1. __Admit__ specific attitudes and actions.

2. __Acknowledge__ the hurt and express regret for all of the harm done.

3. Accompanied by altered attitudes and actions, __turn__ and change in repentance.

NOTES

PEACEMAKING, PART 1: RECONCILING AND AMENDING

If possible, so far as it depends on you, live peaceably with all.

ROMANS 12:18

BEFORE YOU MEET

PRAYERFULLY PREPARE

Spend time in the Scriptures and in the member book, making note of important truths. This way God's Word will be fresh on your heart, providing the truth necessary to keep the session on track.

THIS WEEK'S SCRIPTURES

Day 1: *Ezekiel 14:1-8*

Day 2: *2 Corinthians 5:11-21*

Day 3: *1 Corinthians 13*

Day 4: *Ephesians 5*

Day 5: *Matthew 5:23-26; Numbers 5:5-7; Luke 15:18-19*

Day 6: *Matthew 5:23-24*

NOTES

_____

_____

_____

_____

_____

_____

_____

GOING DEEPER—*To Be Discussed with Mentors*
Identify key questions to supplement the small-group discussion, if needed.

1. How does fear prevent you from loving others as Christ does? Give specific examples from your life (confronting difficult situations, willingness to share your faith, etc.).
2. Have you ever used your knowledge and intellect as a source of pride to beat people down rather than build them up? Give examples.
3. Describe times when your idolatry has distorted your judgment in acting according to God's will.
4. In Matthew 5:23-24 the Lord taught the importance of being reconciled prior to bringing our gifts before the altar. Describe situations in which you offended someone with whom you need to be reconciled.
5. Are there people or institutions to whom you are unwilling to confess and make restitution? Be specific.

WEEK 9 SUMMARY

YOU HAVE HEARD IT SAID—*Wisdom of the World*
Traditional step 8: We made a list of all persons we had harmed and became willing to make amends to them all.

Traditional step 9: We made direct amends to such people whenever possible, except when to do so would injure them or others.

GOD TELLS US IN HIS WORD—*Wisdom of God*
Redeemed truth from steps 8 & 9: Relationships break down because of sin. If there were no sin in the world, relationships would work harmoniously, evidenced by love and unity. Division among God's people provides opportunities to identify sin and purify the body. The gospel of Jesus Christ brings about justice in a way that the law cannot by inwardly reconciling the very heart of injustice to God. As those forgiven by God, we can humbly approach those affected by our sin and make amends. This change of heart brings glory to God by demonstrating the power of the gospel and reflecting His heart in bringing justice through His reconciled people.

WHEN YOU MEET

MINISTRY—*Session Goal*

The goal of this session is to lead participants to confess whom they must seek reconciliation with; to identify the fears, concerns, and challenges in doing so; and to understand how they can seek reconciliation in a way that glorifies God.

■ **PRAYER, ACCOUNTABILITY, & ADMINISTRATION**—*10 minutes*

Begin the session with the following.

- Open in prayer.
- Remind everyone of group guidelines, if necessary.
- Ask whether participants completed their homework.
- Ask whether participants met with their mentors.
- Collect the attendance sheet.

■ **ASK, LISTEN, & REVIEW**—*40 minutes*

Offer help: Communicate that if anyone is struggling with any part of the program, you are available to help after the session.

Foster gospel-centered community through reconciliation: In Christ God has reconciled us to Himself despite our sin. The gospel of Jesus Christ is the only way to truly see reconciliation in the aftermath of sin. The gospel empowers us to humbly seek reconciliation with those we have sinned against.

Questions: In light of what has been reviewed, ask participants:

1. With whom is God asking you to reconcile or make amends?
2. Describe the circumstances and what you should have done differently.
3. What would hinder you from reconciling with those whom you have sinned against?
4. If needed, supplement the discussion with Going Deeper questions.

■ **SPEAK & ENCOURAGE**—*10 minutes*

Use this time to encourage the group, assuring participants that you are for them.

Speak redemptively: Use your reflections from prior sessions and prayer to take participants to Scriptures that speak to their circumstances. Remind them of their identity and of the promises and character of God.

Reintegrate: Emphasize the hope of the gospel from this session's teaching.

> **2 Corinthians 5 :11-21:** We have been made new as representatives of the King acting on behalf of the King under the authority of the King. We have been given a message of hope and love. In all of our relationships we should be thinking, acting and speaking on His behalf.

> **Redeemed truth from steps 8 & 9:** Relationships break down because of sin. If there were no sin in the world, relationships would work harmoniously, evidenced by love and unity. Division among God's people provides opportunities to identify sin and purify the body. The gospel of Jesus Christ brings about justice in a way that the law cannot by inwardly reconciling the very heart of injustice to God. As those forgiven by God, we can humbly approach those affected by our sin and make amends. This change of heart brings glory to God by demonstrating the power of the gospel and reflecting His heart in bringing justice through His reconciled people.

Exhort: Encourage the group to be faithful to do the work by meeting with their mentors and completing the homework for session 9. Encourage them not just to check boxes on their to-do lists but to really seek the Lord.

■ RESPOND—*5 Minutes*
This is an opportunity for members to share something the Spirit is impressing on them, like a confession, a word of encouragement, or a verse.

■ PRAY: COVER WITH THE GOSPEL—*5 Minutes*
As participants are transparent and bare their souls, it is important that we cover them with the gospel in prayer as we conclude.

■ TEACHING—*45–60 Minutes*
Watch the video or transition to a time of teaching.

AFTER YOU MEET

SHEPHERDING TASK

Follow up with participants in the group who are making amends in their relationships with other people. Remind them of their reconciliation with the Lord as they seek to be reconciled with someone else.

NOTES

_____

_____

_____

_____

_____

_____

_____

_____

_____

_____

_____

_____

_____

_____

_____

_____

_____

_____

_____

REFLECTION—*Seeing Through God's Eyes*

A prayerful time of reflection will help lead you to speak redemptively into the lives of group members. This is an ideal time for discipleship as the leader pours into the apprentice leader(s) and then prays for participants.

PRAY FOR GROUP MEMBERS

Ask the Lord to help you see each participant through His eyes and speak redemptively into their situation. The following questions are meant to guide you, but don't feel that you need to answer every question every week or let them limit ways the Lord might speak.

- Where is this person spiritually?
- What areas need healing?
- Were any lies spoken about the truths of God and His character?
- What sinful patterns or strongholds did you discern?
- How could you encourage this person?
- What Scriptures speak to their situation?

NOTES

NOTES

PEACEMAKING, PART 2: CONFRONTING AND FORGIVING

Viewer Guide 10

COMPLETE THIS VIEWER GUIDE AS YOU WATCH THE VIDEO FOR SESSION 10.

Is this an area of wisdom or __preference__, or is this sin?

What is being looked at is the hard-heartedness of being engaged and confronted by a brother who is unwilling to __repent__.

When you see your brother in sin, we, in love, __engage__.

This process of engaging reveals what is already __true__.

In the process of discipline where many are gathered, it is so serious that __Jesus__ Himself is present.

We confront because __God__ confronts us in our sin.

We forgive because we're __forgiven__.

It is possible for us to forgive and not __forget__ the facts.

There's this __intimacy__ in marriage that really requires more forgiveness and more confrontation than any other relationship.

Conflict Wheel

Biblical Peacemaking
Speaking the Truth in Love

Spirit

Avoidant Responses
(Passive/Flight)

Attack Responses
(Aggressive /Fight)

Adapted from Ken Sande, *The Peacemaker* (Grand Rapids, MI: Baker, 2004).

NOTES

_____
_____
_____
_____
_____
_____
_____
_____
_____
_____
_____

PEACEMAKING, PART 2: CONFRONTING AND FORGIVING

Pay attention to yourselves! If your brother sins, rebuke him, and if he repents, forgive him, and if he sins against you seven times in the day, and turns to you seven times, saying, "I repent," you must forgive him.

LUKE 17:3-4

BEFORE YOU MEET

PRAYERFULLY PREPARE

Spend time in the Scriptures and in the member book, making note of important truths. This way God's Word will be fresh on your heart, providing the truth necessary to keep the session on track.

THIS WEEK'S SCRIPTURES

Day 1: *Matthew 18:1-20*

Day 2: *Matthew 18:21-35*

Day 3: *Luke 17:1-10*

Day 4: *Philemon*

Day 5: *Jonah*

Day 6: *Ephesians 4:1-16*

NOTES

_____

_____

_____

_____

_____

GOING DEEPER—*To Be Discussed with Mentors*
Identify key questions to supplement the small group-discussion, if needed.

1. As people repent and confess sin to us, we need to be ready to offer forgiveness. Our forgiveness is evidence that Christ's forgiveness has transformed our hearts and that we want them to be reconciled to God. Prayerfully consider and list the names of people whom you might have difficulty forgiving.

2. Are there brothers or sisters in Christ who may have sinned against you and continue to walk in significant unrepentant sin? Prayerfully consider how God is calling you to forgive these people for the sin they committed against you.

3. Now that bitterness, fear, and shame no longer rule you, are there people outside the body of Christ who may have hurt you and need to be offered peace with God through the blood of Christ?

4. Where are you stuck? Discuss with your group any situations in which you are unwilling to make amends, forgive, confront, or share the gospel. Why?

5. Discuss any fears you have in making amends, forgiving, confronting someone's sin, or sharing the hope of the gospel. Why are you afraid?

6. Are there any relationships you believe are beyond repair?

7. Spend time in prayer as a group, specifically for those situations.

8. Discuss any other questions or issues you are facing.

WEEK 10 SUMMARY

YOU HAVE HEARD IT SAID—*Wisdom of the World*
Traditional step 8: We made a list of all persons we had harmed and became willing to make amends to them all.

Traditional step 9: We made direct amends to such people whenever possible, except when to do so would injure them or others.

GOD TELLS US IN HIS WORD—*Wisdom of God*
Additional redeemed truth from steps 8 & 9: As ambassadors of Christ, we are to be instruments of grace as we confront those who sin against us. We hand our offenses over to God and extend eager forgiveness to those who ask for it. And in this way, fellowship with God and among His people is preserved.

WHEN YOU MEET

MINISTRY—*Session Goal*
The goal of this session is to lead participants to confess where pride and fear of man have caused them not to forgive or confront.

■ PRAYER, ACCOUNTABILITY, & ADMINISTRATION—*10 minutes*
Begin the session with the following.

- Open in prayer.
- Remind everyone of group guidelines, if necessary.
- Ask whether participants completed their homework.
- Ask whether participants met with their mentors.
- Collect the attendance sheet.

■ ASK, LISTEN, & REVIEW—*40 minutes*
Offer help: Communicate that if anyone is struggling with any part of the program, you are available to help after the session.

Foster gospel-centered community through forgiveness: In Christ God has forgiven us of our sin and has imputed Jesus' righteousness to us. Because of the forgiveness we have received because of Jesus, we are able to genuinely forgive others when they sin against us.

Questions: In light of what has been reviewed, ask participants:

1. In what ways do your current relationships reflect Christ's vision for His people? In what ways do they fall short?
2. How do you handle conflict? Are you gracious and gentle, passive or aggressive?
3. What would hinder you from confronting or forgiving people who have sinned against you?
4. If needed, supplement the discussion with Going Deeper questions.

■ SPEAK & ENCOURAGE—*10 minutes*

Use this time to encourage the group, assuring participants that you are for them.

Speak redemptively: Use your reflections from prior sessions and prayer to take participants to Scriptures that speak to their circumstances. Remind them of their identity and of the promises and character of God.

Reintegrate: Emphasize the hope of the gospel from this session's teaching.

> **Matthew 18:** We are the body of Christ; therefore, we should reflect His heart in the way we relate to one another as we work together for His purposes. He desires unity among His people. We are to pursue one another in love and take seriously God's call to holiness. If we fail to address sin, it is impossible to be the redemptive community that He has called us to be.

> **Additional redeemed truth from steps 8 & 9:** As ambassadors of Christ, we are to be instruments of grace as we confront those who sin against us. We hand our offenses over to God and extend eager forgiveness to those who ask for it. And in this way, fellowship with God and among His people is preserved.

Exhort: Encourage the group to be faithful to do the work by meeting with their mentors and completing the homework for session 10. Encourage them not just to check these off their to-do lists but to really seek the Lord

■ RESPOND—*5 minutes*

This is an opportunity for members to share something the Spirit is impressing on them, like a confession, a word of encouragement, or a verse.

■ PRAY: COVER WITH THE GOSPEL—*5 minutes*

As participants are transparent and bare their souls, it is important that we cover them with the gospel in prayer as we conclude.

■ TEACHING—*45–60 minutes*

Watch the video or transition to a time of teaching.

AFTER YOU MEET

SHEPHERDING TASK

Reach out to any participants who seem disconnected from the group and/or anyone in your life whom you might need to confront or forgive.

NOTES

_____

_____

_____

_____

_____

_____

_____

_____

_____

_____

_____

_____

_____

_____

_____

_____

_____

_____

_____

REFLECTION—*Seeing Through God's Eyes*

A prayerful time of reflection will help lead you to speak redemptively into the lives of group members. This is an ideal time for discipleship as the leader pours into the apprentice leader(s) and then prays for participants.

PRAY FOR GROUP MEMBERS

Ask the Lord to help you see each participant through His eyes and speak redemptively into their situation. The following questions are meant to guide you, but don't feel that you need to answer every question every week or let them limit ways the Lord might speak.

- Where is this person spiritually?
- What areas need healing?
- Were any lies spoken about the truths of God and His character?
- What sinful patterns or strongholds did you discern?
- How could you encourage this person?
- What Scriptures speak to their situation?

NOTES

_____

_____

_____

_____

_____

_____

_____

_____

_____

_____

_____

_____

NOTES

_____

_____

_____

_____

_____

_____

_____

_____

_____

_____

_____

_____

_____

_____

_____

_____

_____

_____

_____

_____

_____

_____

PERSEVERING AND PURSUING

Viewer Guide 11

The gospel is continuing to create __*joy*__ and __*faith*__ within us to continue.

Joy: deep, overwhelming, even painful __*longing*__ and yearning for something near yet unattained, tinged with unwavering __*hope*__

Joy is the result of our pursuit of __*Christ*__ .

__*Union*__ with Christ is the foundation of our joy.

UNION WITH CHRIST

1. We're growing in increasing __*like-mindedness*__ to Christ.
2. It shapes how we see the world and pursue __*treasure*__ .

    Christ becomes my __*treasure*__ .

SPIRITUAL DISCIPLINES

- The __*Word*__ of God
- __*Prayer*__
- __*Fasting*__
- __*Rest*__
- __*Service*__

3. We __*persevere*__ with a sense of an enduring joy.

    The __*Spirit*__ is at work to help you persevere.

PERSEVERING THROUGH SUFFERING

1. We must __*reshape*__ our understanding of suffering and trials.
2. We must see that persevering through suffering is an element that is found in __*Christ*__ .

There's this understanding of persevering that I can endure the loss of things, the trial of things, the pain of things, that I might be able to __*know*__ Him better.

In persevering, for the believer, there is a __*joy*__ that comes in knowing and pursuing Him.

Pursuing Treasure

Dependence/Slavery — Position, Physique, Power, People, Personality, Prosperity, Possessions, Posterity → **Christ** → Posterity, Possessions, Prosperity, Personality, People, Power, Physique, Position — Stewardship/Freedom

---

NOTES

_____

_____

_____

_____

_____

_____

_____

_____

_____

_____

_____

WEEK 11

PERSEVERING AND PURSUING

I count everything as loss because of the surpassing worth of knowing Christ Jesus my Lord. For his sake I have suffered the loss of all things and count them as rubbish, in order that I may gain Christ and be found in him, not having a righteousness of my own that comes from the law, but that which comes through faith in Christ, the righteousness from God that depends on faith.

PHILIPPIANS 3:8-9

BEFORE YOU MEET

PRAYERFULLY PREPARE

Spend time in the Scriptures and in the member book, making note of important truths. This way God's Word will be fresh on your heart, providing the truth necessary to keep the session on track.

THIS WEEK'S SCRIPTURES

Day 1:   *Hebrews 12:1-17; James 1:2-18*

Day 2:   *Philippians 3*

Day 3:   *1 Corinthians 9:24-27; Matthew 6:1-18*

Day 4:   *Psalm 63; Ephesians 5:15-21*

Day 5:   *Galatians 5*

Day 6:   *Luke 8:4-15*

NOTES

_____

_____

_____

_____

_____

GOING DEEPER—*To Be Discussed with Mentors*
Identify key questions to supplement the small-group discussion, if needed.

1. What sin or weight do you need to lay aside in order to run the race well?
2. What trials are you facing in your life? In what ways are you tempted to preempt God's purposes of sanctification while under trial?
3. How do you know when you are walking by the Spirit? How does this walk express itself in your life with the people and circumstances you encounter (family, coworkers, children, prayer life, etc.)?
4. What would obedience to Christ look like in your life?
5. When you are thirsting in the wilderness, where do you turn for satisfaction? What does this response reveal about your heart?
6. On what do you tend to obsess, fantasize, meditate, or dwell? Be specific. What is the result (fear, anxiety, depression, worship, praise, joy, etc.)?
7. What stirs your affection for Christ?
8. Being undisciplined leads to laziness or apathy. How disciplined are you in engaging spiritual disciplines daily? If you are undisciplined, why?
9. What does a disciplined life look like specifically for you?
10. What are your goals and motivations for living a disciplined life?
11. Are there things you need to say no to in order to love the Lord and in turn love your spouse, family, friends, neighbors, and coworkers?

WEEK II SUMMARY

YOU HAVE HEARD IT SAID—*Wisdom of the World*
Traditional step 10: We continued to take personal inventory and, when we were wrong, promptly admitted it.

Traditional step 11: We sought through prayer and meditation to improve our conscious contact with God, praying only for the knowledge of His will and the power to carry that out.

GOD TELLS US IN HIS WORD *Wisdom of God*
Redeemed truth from steps 10 & 11: We continue in the fear of the Lord, putting to death those things that rob our affections for Christ while persevering in our loving and joyful obedience to Him. We return to the Lord quickly with an attitude of repentance, when out of step with the Spirit, as we're trained in godliness and grow

spiritually. Since He is our ultimate treasure, we seek to know Him and fill ourselves with those things that stir our affections for Him. We practice spiritual disciplines so that our hearts, so prone to wander, might stay in rhythm with His.

WHEN YOU MEET

MINISTRY—*Session Goal*

The goal of this session is to lead participants to confess areas of their lives in which their actions do not demonstrate their pursuit of God and the glorification of His kingdom.

◼ PRAYER, ACCOUNTABILITY, & ADMINISTRATION—*10 minutes*

Begin the session with the following.

- Open in prayer.
- Remind everyone of group guidelines, if necessary.
- Ask whether participants completed their homework.
- Ask whether participants met with their mentors.
- Collect the attendance sheet.

◼ ASK, LISTEN, & REVIEW—*40 minutes*

Offer help: Communicate that if anyone is struggling with any part of the program, you are available to help after the session.

Foster gospel-centered community through justice: At the cross Jesus absorbed the wrath of God. His death and resurrection delivered us from the wrath to come. God's justice and mercy were demonstrated in response to our injustice. Now that we have been redeemed, God calls us to seek His justice on behalf of those who suffer injustice.

Questions: In light of what has been reviewed, ask participants:

1. What are you pursuing through the use of your time, gifts, and resources?
2. We pursue the things we love. If someone examined your pursuits, what would they conclude about your greatest treasure?
3. How would your life look different if you fully pursued God? What would change if Christ were your treasure and the expansion of His kingdom were your goal?

4. If needed, supplement the discussion with Going Deeper questions.

■ SPEAK & ENCOURAGE—*10 minutes*

Use this time to encourage the group, assuring participants that you are for them.

Speak redemptively: Use your reflections from prior sessions and prayer to take participants to Scriptures that speak to their circumstances. Remind them of their identity and of the promises and character of God.

Reintegrate: Emphasize the hope of the gospel from this session's teaching.

> **Ephesians 5:18:** We have been made alive in Jesus Christ. We have been given the Holy Spirit. We have a responsibility to "be filled with the Spirit" and to nourish our spiritual lives so that our worship motivates our ministry to those around us.

> **Redeemed truth from steps 10 & 11:** We continue in the fear of the Lord, putting to death those things that rob our affections for Christ while persevering in our loving and joyful obedience to Him. We return to the Lord quickly with an attitude of repentance, when out of step with the Spirit, as we're trained in godliness and grow spiritually. Since He is our ultimate treasure, we seek to know Him and fill ourselves with those things that stir our affections for Him. We practice spiritual disciplines so that our hearts, so prone to wander, might stay in rhythm with His.

Exhort: Encourage the group to be faithful to do the work by meeting with their mentors and completing the homework for session 11. Encourage them not just to check these off their to-do lists but to really seek the Lord.

■ RESPOND—*5 minutes*

This is an opportunity for members to share something the Spirit is impressing on them, like a confession, a word of encouragement, or a verse.

■ PRAY: COVER WITH THE GOSPEL—*5 minutes*

As participants are transparent and bare their souls, it is important that we cover them with the gospel in prayer as we conclude.

■ TEACHING—*45–60 minutes*

Watch the video or transition to a time of teaching.

AFTER YOU MEET

SHEPHERDING TASK

Using Stones and Next Steps, which follows session 12 in this leader guide, reach out to group members and encourage them to serve in their church as *Steps* mentors and/or to connect elsewhere in the body of Christ. Recommend participants who might be qualified to lead *Steps* to your pastors and ministers.

NOTES

_____

_____

_____

_____

_____

_____

_____

_____

_____

_____

_____

_____

_____

_____

_____

_____

REFLECTION—*Seeing Through God's Eyes*

A prayerful time of reflection will help lead you to speak redemptively into the lives of group members. This is an ideal time for discipleship as the leader pours into the apprentice leader(s) and then prays for participants.

PRAY FOR GROUP MEMBERS

Ask the Lord to help you see each participant through His eyes and speak redemptively into their situation. The following questions are meant to guide you, but don't feel that you need to answer every question every week or let them limit ways the Lord might speak.

- Where is this person spiritually?
- What areas need healing?
- Were any lies spoken about the truths of God and His character?
- What sinful patterns or strongholds did you discern?
- How could you encourage this person?
- What Scriptures speak to their situation?

NOTES

_____

_____

_____

_____

_____

_____

_____

_____

_____

_____

_____

_____

_____

NOTES

THE JOY OF MAKING MUCH OF HIS NAME

Viewer Guide 12

COMPLETE THIS VIEWER GUIDE AS YOU WATCH THE VIDEO FOR SESSION 12.

Joy hasn't met its completion until it's been passed on and __shared__.

God Himself is extending an invitation to enter into His __joy__.

The God of the universe is extending a personal invitation to join Him in His __work__.

God is literally making His appeal through __you__.

Because Jesus' authority is global, His __mission__ is global.

Jesus' __presence__ is global.

The Spirit will come upon you, and you will be My __witnesses__.

You could walk out of __shame__. You could walk out of the bondage of __slavery__ that all of us were born into.

God is inviting you to take this story that He's given you—the story of __redemption__, the story of hope, the story of a God who loves you, cares for you, and has demonstrated His love and His care for you in the sending of His Son.

This message is the greatest invitation to __joy__.

God is extending a generous and genuine invitation to __join__ Him in His work— His work of redemption.

Comprehensive Gospel

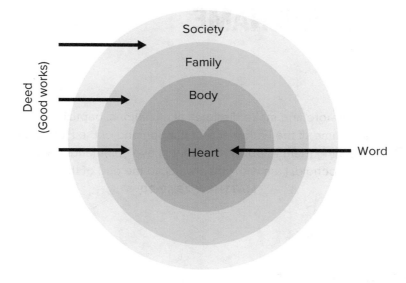

NOTES

_____
_____
_____
_____
_____
_____
_____
_____
_____
_____
_____
_____

THE JOY OF MAKING MUCH OF HIS NAME

Go therefore and make disciples of all nations, baptizing them
in the name of the Father and of the Son and of the Holy Spirit,
teaching them to observe all that I have commanded you.
And behold, I am with you always, to the end of the age.
MATTHEW 28:19-20

BEFORE YOU MEET

PRAYERFULLY PREPARE

Spend time in the Scriptures and in the member book, making note of important truths. This way God's Word will be fresh on your heart, providing the truth necessary to keep the session on track.

THIS WEEK'S SCRIPTURES

Day 1:   *Matthew 28:16-20; Genesis 12:1-3*

Day 2:   *Luke 24:36-53; Acts 1:1-12*

Day 3:   *Ephesians 1:3-14*

Day 4:   *Acts 26*

Day 5:   *Acts 5:12-42*

Day 6:   *John 13:1-19*

NOTES

_____

_____

_____

_____

_____

GOING DEEPER—*To Be Discussed with Mentors*
Identify key questions to supplement the small group-discussion, if needed.

1. How has God blessed you so that you can be a blessing to others?
2. How has God gifted you with spiritual gifts from the Holy Spirit? How will you use those gifts to serve and build up the body of Christ? Be specific.
3. How will you use the testimony of God's grace in your life to guide others toward Christ?
4. Where has God placed you to serve? How do you think others would describe your heart for service?
5. God has called us to make disciples. How will you apply what you have learned through this discipleship process to make disciples for Christ?
6. Acts 17 shows us, through Paul's missionary experiences, that God places us at the exact time and place where He wants to use us. How are you living missionally within your community?
7. How will you continue to practice all you have learned through the *Steps* process? Who will keep you accountable?
8. With what attitude will you engage or reengage with the world around you? Is there any obstacle or excuse that would keep you from doing so?
9. The Book of Joshua recounts the Lord's powerful deliverance of the promised land to the Israelites. As they stepped out in faith, He held back the raging waters of the Jordan River so that they could cross to safety. The Israelites picked up stones from the riverbed to remind them of the Lord's faithfulness. As you have stepped out in faith, in what ways has God demonstrated His faithfulness during this particular season of your life?

WEEK 12 SUMMARY

YOU HAVE HEARD IT SAID *Wisdom of the World*

Traditional step 12: Having had a spiritual experience as the result of these steps, we try to carry this message to others and to practice these principles in all our affairs.

GOD TELLS US IN HIS WORD *Wisdom of God*

Redeemed truth from step 12: Before the foundations of the earth, God chose us, the church, to live as messengers of reconciliation to a lost and dying world, bearing witness to His wisdom and power through the gospel of Jesus Christ. It is our joy-filled worship to make much of His name, empowered by the Holy Spirit in bringing a comprehensive gospel demonstrated by our deeds and proclaimed by our words, with the goal of making disciples for Jesus Christ. In this same way, we incarnate Christ, being His hands and feet on the earth.

WHEN YOU MEET

MINISTRY—*Session Goal*
The goal of this session is to lead participants to discuss what the Word of God says about joy and glorifying God.

■ **PRAYER, ACCOUNTABILITY, & ADMINISTRATION**—*10 minutes*
Begin the session with the following.

- Open in prayer.
- Remind everyone of group guidelines, if necessary.
- Ask whether participants completed their homework.
- Ask whether participants met with their mentors.
- Collect the attendance sheet.

■ **ASK, LISTEN, & REVIEW**—*40 minutes*
Offer help: Communicate that if anyone is struggling with any part of the program, you are available to help after the session.

Foster gospel-centered community through obedience: God calls His people to holiness so that they can reveal His glory to a watching world. Because of Jesus we are free to pursue holiness. Through the Holy Spirit we are empowered to pursue holiness. The promises of God propel us as we seek to love Him and others with the hope of the gospel.

Questions: In light of everything group members have learned and the ways they have grown during the 12 weeks of *Steps,* ask participants:

1. What can you do to make much of the name of Jesus in your current relationships (spouse, friends, neighbors, parents, coworkers, etc)?
2. What tangible next steps can you take to begin making disciples?
3. What significant milestones have you seen in your life because of God's work through *Steps?*
4. If needed, supplement the discussion with Going Deeper questions.

■ SPEAK & ENCOURAGE—*10 minutes*

Use this time to encourage the group, assuring participants that you are for them.

Speak redemptively: Use your reflections from prior sessions and prayer to take participants to Scriptures that speak to their circumstances. Remind them of their identity and of the promises and character of God.

Reintegrate: Emphasize the hope of the gospel from this session's teaching.

> **Matthew 28:16-20:** Carrying forward the idea "Be fruitful and multiply" (Gen. 1:28), Jesus calls us to work to expand His kingdom by making disciples of all nations. As we go, He goes with us.

> **Redeemed truth:** Before the foundations of the earth, God chose us, the church, to live as messengers of reconciliation to a lost and dying world, bearing witness to His wisdom and power through the gospel of Jesus Christ. It is our joy-filled worship to make much of His name, empowered by the Holy Spirit in bringing a comprehensive gospel demonstrated by our deeds and proclaimed by our words, with the goal of making disciples for Jesus Christ. In this same way, we incarnate Christ, being His hands and feet on the earth.

Exhort: Encourage group members to continue seeking the Lord.

■ RESPOND—*5 minutes*

This is an opportunity for members to share something the Spirit is impressing on them, like a confession, a word of encouragement, or a verse.

■ PRAY: COVER WITH THE GOSPEL—*5 minutes*

As participants are transparent and bare their souls, it is important that we cover them with the gospel in prayer as we conclude.

■ TEACHING—*45–60 minutes*

Watch the video or transition to a time of teaching.

AFTER YOU MEET

SHEPHERDING TASK

Follow up with each group member individually to encourage them and pray with them. Share ways you have seen the Lord work during this experience and encourage them to continue pursuing the Lord in a life of obedience. Reach out to your coleader to thank them, pray with them, and encourage them.

NOTES

_____

_____

_____

_____

_____

_____

_____

_____

_____

_____

_____

_____

_____

_____

_____

_____

REFLECTION—*Seeing Through God's Eyes*

A prayerful time of reflection will help lead you to speak redemptively into the lives of group members. This is an ideal time for discipleship as the leader pours into the apprentice leader(s) and then prays for participants.

PRAY FOR GROUP MEMBERS

Ask the Lord to help you see each participant through His eyes and speak redemptively into their situation. The following questions are meant to guide you, but don't feel that you need to answer every question every week or let them limit ways the Lord might speak.

- Where is this person spiritually?
- What areas need healing?
- Were any lies spoken about the truths of God and His character?
- What sinful patterns or strongholds did you discern?
- How could you encourage this person?
- What Scriptures speak to their situation?

NOTES

_____

_____

_____

_____

_____

_____

_____

_____

_____

_____

_____

_____

_____

_____

Stones and Next Steps

STONES OF REMEMBRANCE

God calls His people to remember, celebrate, and tell others about Him. One of these occasions is recorded in the Book of Joshua, when God instructed the Israelites to step into the raging waters of the Jordan River on their way into the promised land. In faith leading to obedience, they stepped in. In a remarkable display of His power, God held back the waters of the Jordan and delivered the whole of Israel safely to the other side. He then instructed them return to the riverbed to pick up stones to serve as a reminder of His deliverance. When their children asked about the stones, they would give the Israelites a reason to share their experience of God's faithfulness.

Similarly, we pick up stones to celebrate God's faithfulness. Many of us stepped out in faith and entered this process fearing that we might be swept away. But God has been faithful to deliver us to the other side. These stones may be personalized with a word, a meaningful Scripture, a date, or a similar reminder so that you can recall what God did during this experience.

WHAT'S NEXT?

Leaders should work with mentors to suggest next steps for participants. Growing disciples of Jesus Christ are involved in gospel-centered worship, gospel-centered community, gospel-centered service, and gospel-centered multiplication. Whether here or at another church, seek to involve participants in each of these ministries. Here are some opportunities.

GOSPEL-CENTERED WORSHIP

We should all have a place we call our church home, where we belong and gather for worship. Gospel-centered worship is the fuel for discipleship. If you are not currently a part of a local church, we encourage you to pursue meaningful membership in a gospel-centered church.

GOSPEL-CENTERED COMMUNITY

We should all be involved relationally with those who live life together in a gospel-centered environment. Such a community provides the context for discipleship. If you are not currently a member of a small group, we encourage you to join a group for mutual encouragement and accountability.

GOSPEL-CENTERED SERVICE

Gospel-centered service is the overflow of discipleship. There are a number of ways to serve in the church. Consider the needs of your church and pursue an opportunity to faithfully serve the Lord and His people.

GOSPEL-CENTERED MULTIPLICATION

Gospel-centered multiplication is the result of discipleship. We encourage you to consider how the Lord is calling you to make disciples.

Consider the following suggestions and options for fulfilling the call to make disciples.

- Now that *Steps* is over, everyone needs to reconnect with the life of the church. Encourage participants who might be qualified to lead or mentor to consider leading a *Steps* group or mentoring a participant in the future. Encourage those who completed *Steps* to continue pursuing gospel-centered community and gospel-centered service.

- Each time your church offers *Steps,* plan to offer a training session that provides a general overview of both *Steps* and the concept of biblical counseling. This training will also allow everyone to learn from one another's experiences and will allow new members and leaders to ask questions and learn from those who have previously completed *Steps*

- The next time your church offers *Steps,* consider having a final extra week as a celebration service. Let this be an opportunity for participants, mentors, and leaders to testify about ways the Lord worked through this process.

- After your mentors have gained adequate training and experience, this *Steps* study can become the foundation for ongoing recovery groups that meet on a regular basis to minister to people who have specific needs.

REDEEMING THE 12 STEPS THROUGH THE GOSPEL

Step 1: We admitted we were powerless over our addictions and compulsive behaviors—that our lives had become unmanageable.

Redeemed truth from step 1: Man, in relationship to his Creator, has fallen from a place of dignity, humility, and dependence to a state of depravity, pride, and rebellion. This has led to unfathomable suffering. Any attempts on our own to redeem ourselves are futile, only increasing the problem of independence and self-sufficiency. Any perceived success leads only to empty vanity. Apart from Christ, we are powerless to overcome sin, and our attempts to control it only increase our chaos.

Step 2: We came to believe that a power greater than ourselves could restore us to sanity.

Redeemed truth from step 2: God lovingly intervened into our chaos and provided a remedy for the insanity of sin and the way back into fellowship with Him. We believe that by grace through faith in Jesus Christ, we can be redeemed.

Step 3: We made a decision to turn our will and our lives over to the care of God, as you understand Him.

Redeemed truth from step 3: Through the Holy Spirit's illumination of our desperate and helpless condition before God and from the hope that comes through the gospel of Jesus Christ, we step out in faith and repent as an act of worship and obedience, surrendering our will and entrusting our lives to Christ's care and control. We are reborn spiritually and rescued from the domain of darkness and brought into the kingdom of light, where we now live as a part of Christ's ever-advancing kingdom.

Step 4: We made a searching and fearless moral assessment of ourselves.

Redeemed truth from step 4: .As children of God armed with the Holy Spirit and standing firm in the gospel, we engage in the spiritual battle over the reign and rule of our hearts. God set us apart for holiness, and we look to put to death the areas of our lives that keep us from reflecting Jesus Christ to a dark and dying world. We first examine the fruit in our lives (or moral symptoms). As we move through the assessment process, we will uncover the roots of any ungodly fruit (pride and idolatry) that drive our ungodly thoughts, actions, and emotions

Step 5: We admitted before God, ourselves, and another human being the exact nature of our wrongs.

Redeemed truth from step 5: Under the covering of God's grace, we step out in faith, leaving behind our old, self-protective ways of covering sin and hiding from God. We prayerfully come into the light, confessing our sins before God and to one another so that we may be healed.

Step 6: We are entirely ready to have God remove all these defects of character.

Step 7: We humbly asked Him to remove our shortcomings.

Redeemed truth from steps 6 & 7: In attempting to live independent of God, we have developed dysfunctional (sinful) patterns of coping. After careful examination we have begun to see the demonic roots of our slavery to these sinful patterns. We desire freedom. We renounce our former ways; offer ourselves to God; and, under the waterfall of His grace, ask Him to deliver and heal us by the authority of Christ and the power of the Holy Spirit. We also pray for blessing and the empowerment of the Holy Spirit to live life according to His kingdom purposes.

Step 8: We made a list of all persons we had harmed and became willing to make amends to them all.

Step 9: We made direct amends to such people whenever possible, except when to do so would injure them or others.

Redeemed truth from steps 8 & 9: Relationships break down because of sin. If there were no sin in the world, relationships would work harmoniously, evidenced by love and unity. Division among God's people provides opportunities to identify sin and purify the body. The gospel of Jesus Christ brings about justice in a way that the law cannot by inwardly reconciling the very heart of injustice to God. As those forgiven by God, we can humbly approach those affected by our sin and make amends. This change of heart brings glory to God by demonstrating the power of the gospel and reflecting His heart in bringing justice through His reconciled people.

Additional redeemed truth from steps 8 & 9: As ambassadors of Christ, we are to be instruments of grace as we confront those who sin against us. We hand our offenses over to God and extend eager forgiveness to those who ask for it. And in this way, fellowship with God and among His people is preserved.

Step 10: We continued to take personal inventory and, when we were wrong, promptly admitted it.

Step 11: We sought through prayer and meditation to improve our conscious contact with God, praying only for the knowledge of His will and the power to carry that out.

Redeemed truth from steps 10 & 11: We continue in the fear of the Lord, putting to death those things that rob our affections for Christ while persevering in our loving and joyful obedience to Him. We return to the Lord quickly with an attitude of repentance, when out of step with the Spirit, as we're trained in godliness and grow spiritually. Since He is our ultimate treasure, we seek to know Him and fill ourselves with those things that stir our affections for Him. We practice spiritual disciplines so that our hearts, so prone to wander, might stay in rhythm with His.

Step 12: Having had a spiritual experience as the result of these steps, we try to carry this message to others and to practice these principles in all our affairs.

Redeemed truth from step 12: Before the foundations of the earth, God chose us, the church, to live as messengers of reconciliation to a lost and dying world, bearing witness to His wisdom and power through the gospel of Jesus Christ. It is our joy-filled worship to make much of His name, empowered by the Holy Spirit in bringing a comprehensive gospel demonstrated by our deeds and proclaimed by our words, with the goal of making disciples for Jesus Christ. In this same way, we incarnate Christ, being His hands and feet on the earth.

APPENDIX B

THE CHARACTER OF GOD

ATTRIBUTE	DESCRIPTION	KEY SCRIPTURES
God is just.	God is right to punish sin.	
God is worthy.	Only God deserves all glory.	
God is generous.	God gives what is best.	
God is Provider.	God meets the needs of His children.	
God is merciful.	God does not give His children the punishment they deserve.	
God is loving.	God does what is best.	
Got is attentive.	God hears and responds to the prayers of His children.	
God is Deliverer.	God rescues His children.	
God is compassionate.	God sees, cares, and acts when His children are in need.	

THE IDENTITY OF A BELIEVER IN UNION WITH JESUS CHRIST

IDENTITY IN CHRIST

Matthew 5:13	I am the salt of the earth.
Matthew 5:14	I am the light of the world.
John 1:12	I am a child of God.
John 15	I am part of the true vine, a branch of Christ's life.
John 15:15	I am a friend of God.
John 15:16	I am chosen and appointed to bear fruit.
Romans 6:5	I am resurrected to new life.
Romans 6:18	I am a slave to righteousness.
Romans 6:22	I am enslaved to God.
Romans 8:14	I am a son of God.
Romans 8:17	I am a joint heir with Christ, sharing his inheritance.
1 Corinthians 6:19	I am the dwelling place of God.
1 Corinthians 6:19	I am united to the Lord.
1 Corinthians 12:27	I am a member of Christ's body.
1 Corinthians 15:10	I am what I am, by God's grace.
2 Corinthians 5:17	I am a new creation.
2 Corinthians 5:18-19	I am reconciled to God.
Galatians 3:29	I am the seed of Abraham.
Galatians 4:6-7	I am an heir of God since I am a son of God.
Ephesians 1:1	I am a saint.
Ephesians 1:3	I am blessed with every spiritual blessing.
Ephesians 2:10	I am God's workmanship, made to do good works.
Ephesians 2:11	I am a fellow citizen of God's family.
Ephesians 4:1	I am a prisoner of Christ.
Ephesians 4:24	I am righteous and holy.
Philippians 3:20	I am a citizen of heaven.
Colossians 3:3	I am hidden with Christ in God.
Colossians 3:4	I am an expression of the life of Christ.
Colossians 3:12	I am chosen of God, holy and dearly loved.
1 Thessalonians 5:5	I am a child of light and not darkness.
Titus 3:7	I am an heir to eternal life.
Hebrews 3:1	I am a holy partaker of a heavenly calling.
1 Peter 2:5	I am a living stone in God's spiritual house.
1 Peter 2:9	I am a member of a chosen race, a holy nation.
1 Peter 2:9-10	I am a priest.

1 Peter 2:11	I am an alien and a stranger to the world.
1 Peter 5:8	I am an enemy of the Devil.
2 Peter 1:3	I am participating in the divine nature.
1 John 5:18	I am born of God, and the Devil cannot touch me.

IDENTITY APART FROM CHRIST

Genesis 6:5	I am wicked and evil.
Isaiah 59:2	I am separated from God.
Isaiah 64:6	I am filthy and stained.
John 8:34	I am a slave to sin.
Romans 1:18	I am under the wrath of God.
Romans 3:10	I am not good.
Romans 3:23	I am falling short of the glory of God.
Romans 6:23	I am guilty and condemned.
2 Corinthians 4:4	I am blind to the truth.
2 Corinthians 11:3	I am deceived.
Ephesians 2:1	I am dead in my sins.
Ephesians 2:2	I am in bondage to Satan.
Ephesians 4:18	I am hard-hearted.
James 2:10	I am a lawbreaker.
James 4:4	I am an enemy of God.

APPENDIX D

GOD'S PROMISES TO A BELIEVER

Matthew 6:25-30	God will provide for your needs.
Matthew 11:28-30	Rest in Christ.
Matthew 21:22	Ask in His name, and you will receive.
Matthew 24:9-14	Persecution is coming.
Matthew 26:29	He is waiting to eat with you.
Matthew 28:20	He is with us always, to the end of age.
Mark 16:16	Whoever believes and is baptized will be saved.
Luke 12:27-34	He knows what you need; seek His kingdom, and what you need will be provided.
John 14:1-4	Jesus is preparing a place for you.
John 14:13-14	Ask in Jesus' name, and He will do it so that the Father can be glorified in the Son.
John 14:27	He gives us His peace.
John 15:7-8	If you remain in Him, ask whatever you want.
John 15:5	If you remain in Christ, you will produce fruit.
John 16:13-15	The Holy Spirit will guide you into all truth.
John 16:23-24	Ask the Father in Jesus' name, and it will be given so that your joy may be full.
Acts 1:8	You will receive power when the Holy Spirit comes.
Acts 2:38-39	The promise is for you, the believer.
Romans 6:14	Sin will not rule over you.
Romans 8:27	The Holy Spirit intercedes for the saints according to the will of God.
Romans 8:34	Jesus is at the right hand of the Father interceding for you.
Romans 8:39	Nothing will have the power to separate you from the love of God in Jesus Christ.
1 Corinthians 1:8	He will strengthen you till the end.
1 Corinthians 2:13	The Holy Spirit will teach you.
1 Corinthians 2:16	You have been given the mind of Christ.
1 Corinthians 10:13	God will not allow you to be tempted beyond what you are able, and He will provide a way out.
1 Corinthians 15:52-57	You will be raised into an incorruptible immortal body at the resurrection of the dead.
2 Corinthians 3:18	You are being transformed into the image of Christ.
Philippians 1:6	He who started a good work in you will complete it.

Philippians 3:21	He will transform the body of our humble condition into the likeness of His glorious body.
Philippians 4:7	The peace of God will guard your heart and mind in Jesus Christ.
1 Thessalonians 5:24	He who calls you is faithful, who will also do it.
2 Thessalonians 3:3	The lord is faithful and will strengthen and guard you from the Evil One.
Titus 3: 6-7	He has abundantly poured out His Spirit on us through Jesus, and we are heirs to the hope of eternal life.
Hebrews 7:25	He is able to save all who come to Him, and He always intercedes for them.
Hebrews 8:8-12	God will never again remember your sins.
Hebrews 10:16-17	In the new covenant God will never again remember your sins or your lawless acts.
Hebrews 13:5	God will never leave or forsake you.
1 Peter 1:3-5	Inheritance is imperishable, undefiled, uncorrupted, unfading, kept in heaven for you.
1 Peter 2:10	You are now a part of God's people.
Revelation 21:1-7	God will dwell with us and wipe away every tear, and death will no longer exist.

DEFINITIONS OF CHARACTER DEFECTS

Abuse: To treat wrongly or harmfully

Addiction: The condition of being habitually or compulsively occupied with or involved in something

Adultery: Voluntary sexual intercourse between a married person and a partner other than the lawful spouse

Anger: A strong feeling of displeasure or hostility

Anxiety: A state of apprehension, uncertainty, and fear resulting from the anticipation of a realistic or fantasized threatening event or situation, often impairing physical and psychological functioning

Bitterness: Unresolved anger and ill will

Bigotry: Hatred of people who are different from me in a clearly definable way, such as race, gender, or political affiliation

Busyness/overscheduling: Planning too many activities in my life so that I do not have time to think about my life

Condemnation: Strong displeasure or judgment

Coveting: Having a desire for another's possessions, power, wealth, or relationships

Critical: Judging, blaming, or finding fault with someone or something

Death/suicide: Enticement to take one's own life or fanaticizing about death

Defeated: Believing there is no hope of victory

Defensive/self-justification: Giving a good reason for my actions; showing my behavior to be just or right; clearing myself from blame for my actions or attitudes

Denial: A false systems of beliefs that are not based on reality; self-protecting behavior that keeps me from honestly facing the truth

Deceitful: Lying, cheating, or stealing; not upright in my dealings with people

Depression: The condition of being lowered in spirit; dejected

Detachment: To remove from association (from self or others); dissociation

Doubt: To be undecided or skeptical

Entitlement: Deserving of rights or benefits

Envy: Wishing to have something someone else has; disliking someone who has more than I do

Fear: A feeling that makes you turn away or run from something

Gluttony: Excess in any area, particularly in eating or drinking; greedy

Gossiping: Idle talk, not always true, about other people and their lives

Grandiosity: Having or showing too great an opinion of my importance

Greed: Wanting more than my fair share

Guilt: Remorseful awareness of having done something wrong

Hate: A feeling of intense anger or bitterness; extreme dislike toward someone; a feeling of intense ill will toward another person

Hoarding: Saving money of things in excess; storing up more than could reasonably be used

Impatience: Annoyance because of delay or opposition

Intolerance: Unwillingness to allow others to have opinions or beliefs that are different from mine

Jealousy: Dislike or fear of rivals; envy; anxious or suspicious watchfulness

Lack of trust: Not being able to trust; not being able to depend on someone or something; doubt; lack in belief in God's goodness

Laziness: Dislike of work; unwillingness to work or be active

Legalism: Strict adherence to rules of conduct without regard to the principles behind them; dependence on my behavior for my sense of self-worth

Licentiousness: Lacking moral discipline or ignoring legal restraint

Lust: Strong desire; unhealthy appetite of desire, especially in the area of sexual indulgences

Lying: Not telling the truth; exaggerating; boasting

Mania: An excessively elevated sense of enthusiasm, interest, or desire; a craze

Minimizing: Making excuses for or making less of my behavior to make myself and others think I am not "that bad"

Negative thinking: Always thinking on the bad side of a situation; refusing to see good in anything that happens; not looking at things from God's point of view

Obsession: Overwhelming attention to a particular thought, action, or person that you cannot escape

Oppression: The act of subjugating by cruelty or force or the state of being subjugated this way

Passivity: Accepting ideas without giving them any thought; failing to act when action is needed

People pleasing: Doing activities based on the positive reactions of people around me; making myself feel better by getting the approval of someone else

Perfectionism: Working to arrange my life so that everything and everyone in it is faultless, according to my standards

Pettiness: Focusing on the small, meaningless things in my life; giving those things more importance than they deserve

Phoniness: Deceiving; being insincere; not being genuine; also includes emotional phoniness

Pride: Too high opinion of myself; high opinion of my worth or possessions

Procrastination: Putting off to a future date something I feel I should have done sooner to avoid unpleasant or undesirable consequences

Quarrelsome: Too quick to find fault; fond of fighting and disputing

Resentment: Sulking; vindictiveness (getting even); reliving emotional hurts and pain

Sarcasm: A sneering or cutting remark; the act of making fun of someone to hurt their feelings; harsh or bitter irony

Self-pity: To feel sorry for myself, to live in regret of my past actions; continually reviewing my miseries, often blaming others for my troubles

Self-centeredness: Being overly concerned with my welfare or interests; having little or no concern for others; thinking what I want is the most important thing

Selfishness: Caring too much for myself and too little for those around me

Shame: A painful emotion caused by a strong sense of guilt, embarrassment, unworthiness, or disgrace

Undisciplined: Untrained; lack of order; lack of self control; disobedient; impulsive

Vulgar thinking: Immoral thinking about things that are unhealthy or immoral; making a practice of dwelling on these thoughts for pleasure or comfort

THE INSANITY CYCLE OF SIN

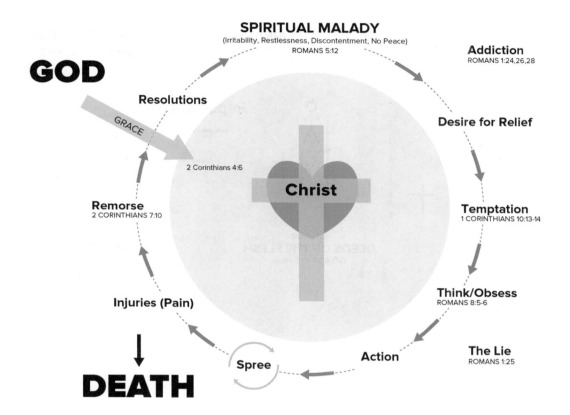

APPENDIX G

THE THREE CIRCLES: A GOD-CENTERED LIFE

Fallen Man

Chaos

- SELF-CENTERED/SELFISH
- SELF-SEEKING (FEAR)
- SELF-RELIANT (POWER)
- OBSESSED WITH CONTROL, OTHERS, CIRCUMSTANCES
- SPIRITUAL—ALIVE TO SIN, DEAD TO GOD

Christian Walking by the Flesh

Repentance

Fear/Lust

Chaos
DEEDS OF THE FLESH
GALATIANS 5:19-21

Christian Walking by the Spirit

Order
FRUIT OF THE SPIRIT
GALATIANS 5:22-23

- GOD-CENTERED SERVANT
- GOD-PLEASING (FAITH)
- DEPENDENT ON MY CREATOR
- SURRENDERED TO GOD'S SOVEREIGNTY

Adapted from Campus Crusade for Christ.

APPENDIX H

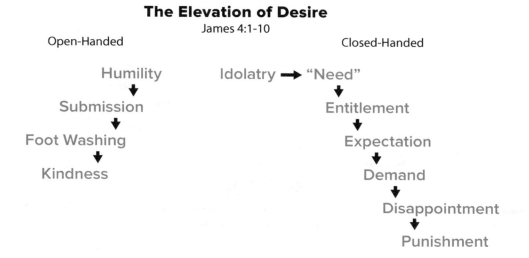

The Elevation of Desire
James 4:1-10

Open-Handed   Closed-Handed

Humility   Idolatry → "Need"

Submission   Entitlement

Foot Washing   Expectation

Kindness   Demand

Disappointment

Punishment

Paul David Tripp, *War of Words: Getting to the Heart of Your Communication Struggles* (Phillipsburg, NJ: P&R Publishing, 2000), 59.

APPENDIX I

Getting to the Roots of Ungodly Fruit and Character Defects

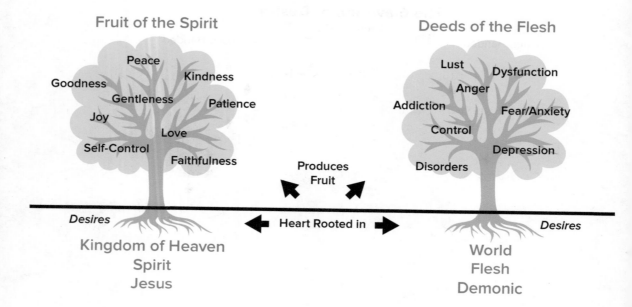

Fruit of the Spirit

Peace
Kindness
Goodness
Gentleness
Patience
Joy
Love
Self-Control
Faithfulness

Deeds of the Flesh

Lust
Dysfunction
Anger
Addiction
Fear/Anxiety
Control
Depression
Disorders

Produces Fruit

Desires   Heart Rooted in   Desires

Kingdom of Heaven
Spirit
Jesus

World
Flesh
Demonic

Salvation

Accomplished

Foundations
of the Earth

Birth

Conversion
(Rebirth)

Death or
Christ's Return

Law

Grace

Eternity

Faith

Glorified

Foreknew/
Predestined

Called

Sanctified

Justified/Adopted

NOTES

NOTES

WHERE TO GO FROM HERE

Now that you've completed this study, here are a few possible directions you can go for your next one.

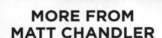

MORE FROM MATT CHANDLER

HOLY SPIRIT

DISCIPLESHIP

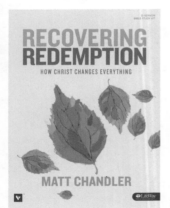

Discover the root of brokenness and destructive patterns of behavior, and see how the gospel is the remedy to fix all things. (12 sessions)

Go beyond the doctrines you already know to the Person Jesus wants you to know. (8 sessions)

Understand the basic concepts behind following Jesus in the modern world, and learn to share these truths with others. (5 sessions)